Praise for Messy Beautiful Love

"In an age when wives often pride themselves on being right, Darlene shows the power of *doing* right. The timeless truth in this book will help any marriage."

— ARLENE PELLICANE
author of *31 Days to Becoming a Happy Wife*

"I love Darlene's writing! This book both challenges and motivates me to exchange God's ideas and ideals for my own. Her hope-filled story of a marriage changed by the grace of God reminds us that no marriage is ever beyond God's redeeming grace."

— COURTNEY JOSEPH
author of *Women Living Well* and the blog *WomenLivingWell.org*

"Life is messy. Relationships are messy. And marriage is a beautiful messy blend of both! Yet with Christ as our Messiah, those messes can become a mosaic of grace, hope, wonder, and redemption!"

— RENEE SWOPE
best-selling author of *A Confident Heart*, Proverbs 31 Ministries radio cohost, and blogger at *ReneeSwope.com*

"Most of us will agree that marriage can be messy at times. Even the strongest, most intentional ones. Darlene doesn't dwell on the disarray we often selfishly create. Instead, she poignantly spurs us on to embrace hope in the ups and downs. She reminds us that when we shift our focus from ourselves to Jesus and His perfect work on the cross, our marriages can indeed be beautiful."

ASHLEIGH SLATER
author of *Team Us: Marriage Together*

"Marriage is . . . messy, beautiful love! The greatest message in this book is the amazing grace that can be experienced between a husband and wife, true love among the messes. Darlene's marriage is inspiring and fills people with hope because it is a powerful testimony of God's amazing grace."

— JENNIFER SMITH
author of *Wife After God* and
UnveiledWife.com

"It's easy to be pulled in by the chorus (friends, media) of voices that say, 'Marriage is hard and it will never get better,' but Darlene challenges you to live beyond those messages and embrace a new mantra, 'Marriage may be hard, but it can also be extraordinary.' She challenges you to rise to God's plan for your marriage, not sink into the mediocrity of the world's expectations. Highly recommended."

— KATHI LIPP
speaker, and author of *The
Husband Project* and *The Cure for
the "Perfect" Life*

"Darlene writes with authenticity leading us to discover a life-changing truth: a beautiful marriage is not only possible, it's inevitable when a wife is transformed by the wisdom of God. Thank you, Darlene, for a powerful and honest look at a God-centered marriage."

— LYNN DONOVAN
author of *Winning Him Without
Words* and *Not Alone: Trusting God
to Help You Raise Godly Kids in a
Spiritually Mismatched Home*

"Obedience to God's plan for each of our lives in marriage can get us through any bump we may encounter along the road of love and faith. I couldn't help but ask myself 'how many marriages might be saved if this book and its message were sincerely read and taken to heart?'"

— NAOMI STRIEMER
Christian Contemporary singer,
speaker, and best-selling author

"Marriage is messy. Appliances get broken. Sometimes promises do too. Clutter happens—both in our homes and our hearts. Soon our happily-ever-after turns into a 'what was I thinking?' Darlene's honest and insightful look—at both our role and at God's—will empower you and your spouse to carefully craft a marriage that truly glorifies Him."

— KAREN EHMAN
Proverbs 31 Ministries; author
of seven books including *Let. It.
Go. How to Stop Running the Show
and Start Walking in Faith* and
Everyday Confetti

"Darlene writes in such a powerful and yet gentle way that I couldn't help but be moved—and challenged—as she so effectively captures both the beauty and messiness of real love. Whether you're newly married or have been married for many years, you will find *Messy Beautiful Love* an inspiring and compelling book to read again and again."

— LISA JACOBSON
author of *100 Ways to Love Your
Husband*

"God took Darlene's mess and made it beautiful. Now she's calling other women to follow not her but Jesus as He helps us find peace, joy, and contentment—even in our own messes."

— SHEILA WRAY GREGOIRE
author of *The Good Girl's Guide
to Great Sex* and blogger at
tolovehonorandvacuum.com

"*Messy Beautiful Love* touches on real marital topics, which are meaningful and quite common, but are unfortunately often discarded. Darlene gives excellent biblical wisdom on how God *can* get the glory out of the seemingly impossible marriage."

— JANELLE M. NEHRENZ
author of *Comfy in the Kitchen*

"Darlene weaves a story of mercy, putting others before ourselves, laying down the need to be right, and, above all, loving even when we don't feel like it. It's the gospel, really, wrapped up in a story about redeemed marriage. It's how God loves us, and how He can help us love our spouses."

— BROOKE MCGLOTHLIN
cofounder of the MOB Society
(for mothers of boys) and author of
Praying for Boys: Asking God for the Things They Need Most

MESSY
Beautiful
LOVE

MESSY
Beautiful
LOVE

DARLENE SCHACHT

NELSON
BOOKS
An Imprint of Thomas Nelson

Published in Nashville, Tennessee, by Nelson Books, an imprint of Thomas Nelson. Nelson Books and Thomas Nelson are registered trademarks of HarperCollins Christian Publishing, Inc.

Thomas Nelson titles may be purchased in bulk for educational, business, fund-raising, or sales promotional use. For information, please e-mail SpecialMarkets@ ThomasNelson.com.

Unless otherwise noted, Scripture quotations are taken from the King James Version.

Scripture quotations marked NKJV are taken from THE NEW KING JAMES VERSION. © 1982 by Thomas Nelson, Inc. Used by permission. All rights reserved.

Scripture quotations marked NLT are taken from Holy Bible, New Living Translation. © 1996, 2004, 2007. Used by permission of Tyndale House Publishers, Inc., Wheaton, Illinois 60189. All rights reserved.

Scripture quotations marked ESV are taken from the English Standard Version. © 2001 by Crossway Bibles, a division of Good News Publishers.

Scripture quotations marked NIV are taken from the Holy Bible, New International Version`, NIV`. Copyright © 1973, 1978, 1984, 2011 by Biblica, Inc.™ Used by permission of Zondervan. All rights reserved worldwide. www.zondervan.com

Library of Congress Cataloging-in-Publication Data

Schacht, Darlene.
  Messy beautiful love : hope and redemption for real-life marriages / Darlene Schacht.
    pages cm
  Includes bibliographical references.
  ISBN 978-1-4002-0620-9
  1. Marriage—Religious aspects—Christianity. I. Title.
  BV835.S33 2014
  248.8'44—dc23   2014004901

Printed in the United States of America

14 15 16 17 18 19 RRD 6 5 4 3 2 1

*To Michael, you have shown me the
beauty of true and lasting love.*

Contents

CONTENTS

Foreword

MARRIAGE.

There's no relationship like it on earth. In the good times, it makes our hearts dance with joy, and in the bad times, it can take us to the pit of despair.

Loving our husbands through the hard times, through the valleys, and when they are most unlovable, reveals the gospel in our lives. It shows we are true followers of Christ as we love unconditionally and lay our lives down for another.

Many go into marriage thinking about what they can take out of the relationship. They are "me" focused, and when the marriage fails to give "me" an immediate return, they treat the marriage like it's expendable.

Sweet wives, you hold a precious title. The title of Wife! Social confusion, discontentment, and dissatisfaction will bring us down if we do not rise above them through the power of God and His Word.

According to Proverbs 31:10, a good wife is of exceptional worth. We hold a vital role in the lives of our husbands. And though it's been seventeen years since my wedding bells rang and the butterflies are a lot less frequent, the depth of love, from embracing our roles written out in Scripture, knows no bounds. It multiplies exponentially every year!

It is by far the best investment I've made in my life, and each time I invest my time, energy, heart, and soul into my marriage, I continue to reap a return on my investment.

This book Darlene has written both challenges and motivates me to exchange God's ideas and ideals for my own. Her hope-filled story of a marriage changed by the grace of God reminds us that no marriage is ever beyond God's redeeming grace.

Join her on this journey as she *tunes out* the world's noise and *tunes in* to the Creator of marriage.

Walk with the King,
Courtney Joseph, author of the
book *Women Living Well* and
the blog *WomenLivingWell.org*

Introduction

GROWING UP IN THE 1970S, I WATCHED AS my parents struggled to make their way through life and battled to keep their marriage alive. Sometimes they battled each other, but most often they were fighting against the weight of the world. Raising six daughters on one income put a financial strain on things, not to mention the fact that they had little time left for themselves or each other.

My rose-colored glasses showed me a different picture when it came to what my life would look like. Captain and Tennille had convinced me that love would keep us together, and why wouldn't it? When two people truly love each other, nothing in this world could threaten that love or come between them. Could it? The problem was that my definition of love was skewed by selfish ambition.

Falling in love with Michael painted another picture for me—one of self-sacrifice. The beauty of marriage isn't based on the fact that we can laugh well together—and believe me, we do—it's that we can also cry well together when life gets us down. I have a partner who is holding my hand through every trial and temptation we face, and while he's got mine, I've got a fierce grip on his.

Life has been messy at times, but I've come to understand that true and incomparable love is a beautiful thing. We have each other to lean on when we both need it most. It's a bit of a struggle some days, but yes, it's worth battling for!

| ONE |

Messy, Beautiful Love

IT WAS MY HUSBAND'S BIRTHDAY. WE HAD plans for the evening, and I was hoping to make his day the best that I could. The presents were waiting, and the kids and I were looking forward to taking Michael to dinner.

Bouncing around the house, I went from the closet to the dresser and back to the closet again, looking for the perfect outfit. You'd think that with a closet the size of Texas I'd find something in there, but it's never that easy. What's supposed to be clean and organized looks like something from an episode of *Hoarders*. I swear that my husband is hanging onto T-shirts that he purchased in high school. And most of the

1

clothes that I have are too small, too formal, or too 1980s to wear. Nothing is ever just right.

Finally deciding on sea green, I pulled a cotton blouse off the hanger and slipped it over my head. The butterfly arms and soft flow of fabric were the perfect solution for hiding the extra ten pounds I'd put on that winter. The sequined front bodice? A special touch for a special occasion!

Looking in the mirror, I wondered whether I should go back to brown hair. I've always had strawberry blonde hair, but there's something about brown hair that makes my eyes look brand new. I'd never really noticed how green my eyes were until I went brown, but like anything else it was hard to get used to a change.

Brown or blonde, I knew the blouse would bring out the color in my eyes. Maybe not brand-new eyes, but I take what I can get! The rest of the outfit was simple. Denim capris are my go-to pants when the weather is nice, and since the day was sunny and warm, the decision to wear them was easy.

Finally pulling my hair into a ponytail, it was mission accomplished. I could have dressed up since it was a special occasion—maybe some heels and a skirt—but I figured that since we'd likely be walking outside, casual was the best way to go.

It's a family tradition that whenever one of us has a birthday, we all go out to eat at a restaurant. Normally Michael picks something that the entire family will like, which often lands us at the Forks Market eating spaghetti and fresh sourdough bread. There's nothing quite like the taste of fresh bread with garlic butter, is there? It's even better when you're enjoying the bread from an old streetcar that's been upcycled to re-create a vintage dining experience. The nostalgic atmosphere is enough to carry anyone back to the Roaring Twenties, but the presence of skater boys with ball caps flipped to the side ensures that we quickly return to the present.

Speaking of presents, I still had some wrapping to do when I heard the hum of the garage door open and close. I glanced at the clock. It was only three thirty; the kids weren't even home from school yet. Michael wasn't due home for at least another hour, and if you know my husband at all, you'll understand why this took me by surprise. Michael's never been late for work, he doesn't come home early, and he'll miss a day only if he's bleeding from the eyes. Whatever the case, I was just glad he was home. This was going to be an awesome night with the family, and I couldn't wait for it to get started!

Leaving his briefcase by the door, he asked me to join him in the living room. I wasn't sure what was up, but one glance at the stone-cold look on his face told me that something was wrong—terribly wrong.

Sitting across from him, I'll never forget the sound of his voice as it rang in my ears and ripped through my heart.

"Are you having an affair?" he asked.

Looking up at him, I quickly answered, "No. Why would you even ask that?"

"Please don't lie to me," he said. As he continued to question me, the heat rose in my face. My cheeks were numb; my mouth was dry; my body was weak. "Did you have an affair?"

I hung my head, unable to look in his eyes. Sitting alone on the couch, I felt the fear of truth spin around me like the web of a spider until I was helpless to move. Barely able to speak, I lifted my chin in a nod and then in another. My house of cards collapsed, my shame crashing to the ground along with it.

My sin, the glorious fruit of lust, had enticed me into the pit where all I could think of was death. For death itself had enveloped me, and with it came shame and reproach. I had sinned against God, my husband, and my family. Everything I had once held so dear to me loomed above the pit of sin and shame I had dug for myself.

Every muscle in my body was heavy, tense, numb. I was disconnected from the pounding of the blood that sped through my head like a runaway train. Even if I wanted to speak—even if I had something else to say—I couldn't. My jaw was locked; my throat was closed.

Michael stood up, and as I watched him walk out of the room, I realized that in every sense of the word, I was alone.

Through a fog of confusing emotions, I managed to get off the couch and go out to the car where I fished through my purse for my keys. Not knowing what else to do, I drove. I didn't know where I was going, what I should do, or where I'd be spending the night. All I knew was that I had to go some-place—anyplace—but where?

Finally pulling into a parking lot, I stopped the car and collapsed onto the steering wheel. My thoughts were a dark and dusty swirl of emotions that ripped through my heart and beckoned me into the grave. Tears poured down my face like poison escaping a wound, and I sobbed until my stomach was raw from the pain.

I didn't have a plan. I didn't have a home. And I didn't have a shoulder to cry on. All that I had were the shattered pieces of my life. A few hours later I made my way back to the house, where I started packing up a few things I could carry. Michael came into the room and sat down on the far corner of the bed. Staring straight ahead, he started to talk. This was my husband, the man I had lived with for nearly half of my life, but in every way he was different, from the sound of his voice to the way that he carried himself. We were suddenly strangers.

We exchanged words for a while, but at the end of the day, I had nothing left to offer him but soiled rags, words of remorse that he couldn't rely on, and promises where all trust was gone. My eyes were swollen from crying; my heart was heavy with shame.

"Do you want to stay?" he asked.

I didn't know how to answer. All I wanted to do was stay with my family—to turn back the clock a year. Back to a time when being a wife and a mom was all that I knew and all that

I wanted to be. But I was unworthy to be a wife, a mother, and a child of God. How could I stay in a place where I didn't belong? How could I ever live on the surface again? How could I ever be trusted to love?

"I can't," I said. "I just can't."

Again he said, "That's not what I'm asking you. Do you *want* to stay?"

Loving his wife as Christ loves the church, Michael reached down to me with a hand of grace when I needed it most. When every thought told me that I was unworthy of love, something miraculous happened that changed the way that I look at marriage and the way that I look at our Savior. It was the realization that I am saved by nothing but the power of grace.

Perhaps that's how the woman who was caught in adultery felt when she was brought to Jesus. Face-to-face with her Savior, she was left with nothing but His hand of grace. What did Jesus write in the sand with His finger that day? Some say He was listing sins—and perhaps He was. But a part of me will always wonder whether it was an invitation that beckoned her to come home to a place where sin is washed away by the blood of an incomparable Savior.

There is incredible power in the words of Jesus Christ, who said, "Neither do I condemn you; go and sin no more" (John 8:11 NKJV). It takes incredible strength for a man to echo those very same words.

I didn't deserve Michael's love and forgiveness. I didn't deserve a second chance. I didn't deserve my family, and I didn't deserve to be loved by those whom I hurt. But in that moment of darkness when one person in this world cared enough to display the covenant-keeping love of Jesus Christ to His church, I turned from my sin and clung to the grace of God that is strong enough to break the bonds of sin and death. It's strong enough to graft one man to a woman when everything in this world threatens to pull them apart.

I was called out from that place of grace while wondering whether God could use the testimony of someone who was broken and tarnished like me. Even after I came to a place of healing, digging this up was the furthest thing from my mind. I wanted nothing more than to encourage women with *joy*; to offer them a Pollyanna view of marriage that brought a smile to their day—housekeeping schedules, adorable printables, and entertaining articles that were easy to swallow with their morning cup of tea. That would be the easy road, but as time went by, I felt an undeniable nudge toward the road less paved—painful honesty.

Painful honesty hardly describes the experience I had when I went to my father's bedside with my sin. He was in the hospital, diagnosed with lung cancer that had metastasized to his brain, which was then riddled with tumors. Barely eighty-five pounds, he peered out from beneath a cloud of yellow blankets as I entered the room. Tears were streaming down my cheeks, and I asked my sister if I could have a few minutes alone with Dad.

Before I continue with this story, let me back up to give you a little history on him. Next to my husband, my dad was the most Christlike man I've ever met. He loved nothing more than to talk about God, and he spent endless hours reading the Bible. During his retirement I'd guesstimate that he read it about fifteen times, which is pretty cool for a man with a grade-three education. His style was to read from Genesis to Revelation and then read again from Revelation to Genesis. He also had an incredible sense of humor, which made him the love of my life.

Aside from the fact that he was battling cancer, I didn't want to disappoint someone who had made it his mission to instill faith in his family. He spent his life being an example to us so that we would come to know the Lord, but there I was with my tear-stained cheeks ready to shatter those dreams.

"What's wrong?" he asked.

Grabbing a spot on the corner of his bed, I started to tell him my story. "I had an affair," I said. My voice was low since he was sharing a room with someone behind the blue curtain.

"What?" he replied, pulling himself up on his pillow.

I answered a little louder this time, "I had an affair."

Dad shook his little head in confusion. "What? I still can't hear you!" he said.

Shouting this time, I repeated my sin: "I had an affair!"

I'm certain that the nurses' station down the hall heard every word, but apparently Dad didn't as he shook his head once again and said, "I'm sorry, but I can't hear what you're saying."

It was time to grab a pen and paper. With trembling hands I wrote down the four words that few dare to speak of and handed them to my father. The room was silent. He studied the paper a moment and then reached out for my hand to pray. "Lord," he said, "I understand that Darlene doesn't think that life is fair. And, God, I pray that You will help her."

What? My mind started racing. *He still doesn't grasp what I'm saying. He thinks I wrote that life isn't fair. What should I do?*

Placing my hand on his arm, I stopped him. "Dad," I said as loudly as I possibly could, "no, I had an affair."

As funny as my dad could be when it came to his hearing, it was a terrifying experience as I sat in his room screaming my sin throughout the halls of St. Boniface Hospital, but I'll tell you one thing I know: following God's lead is *always* worth the risk.

When he finally understood the gravity of what I was saying, he reached for my hand once again and gave me a gift drawn from the well of his wisdom. "God doesn't care about what you did yesterday," he said. "He's concerned about what you'll do today."

There's a good reason why I stepped out of my comfort zone to share the truth of my testimony, and it's the same reason I'm writing this today—so that my marriage will be a testimony of the saving grace of our Lord, Jesus Christ. This testimony of grace is not exclusive to me or you or the sinner-turned-preacher who's standing onstage. It's the testimony of each and every person who takes the hand of another in marriage as we are called to bear witness to the covenant-keeping grace of our Lord: "The husband is the head of the wife, even as Christ is the head of the church: and he is the saviour of the body" (Eph. 5:23).

When marriage functions as God intended it, both a husband and a wife bring glory to God. My mission is to remind women of this truth so that we might live out our purpose, which is to love our husbands, raise our children with intent, and manage our homes well. In doing so, we strengthen the bond of marriage and glorify God.

When I felt the calling to minister to women in this way, it was a humbling experience. I remember sitting in the backyard, sniffling with a tissue in hand as I poured my heart out to Michael. I couldn't process my feelings. On the one hand, I felt this undeniable calling, but on the other, so many questions remained. How could I bring anything of worth? How could I minister to the hearts of women when I had failed so terribly? Why would God use a failure when there are so many strong women of faith?

Michael offered warm words of encouragement and a shoulder to lean on—he's good at that—but I really needed to ask God *why* He was calling.

A few weeks later I was sitting on the couch, typing out an article with a can of diet soda by my side. It was midafternoon, the kids were in school, and the house was quiet, except for the green-cheeked conure who was busy in her cage practicing the "Give me a kiss" voice.

Suddenly out of nowhere and much to my surprise, I heard the voice of God as He spoke to me, saying, "Write this." I paused, and He spoke again, "Write this down."

When the Lord says, "Take dictation," let me tell you, you type! And not only do you type, but you type it word for word.

He continued, "It doesn't matter where you have been or what you have done, My grace is sufficient for you."

I got a little choked up when that sentence came to me so clearly. It's not every day that I get such a clear message. Yet I wondered, *Is it really God instructing me to speak directly to you? Am I really hearing His voice say with authority, "Write this down"?*

Immediately I turned to my devotional for backup. Next to my Bible, I keep this book close and flip it open often. Like a kid tearing off paper on Christmas morning, I was anxious to see what was inside. Turning the pages, I prayed, "God if there is something in here that says, 'My grace is sufficient for you,' I'm going to pass out. Seriously, I don't know what I'll do."

I landed on the page, and no, that's not what it said, but the message He gave me was deeper and more explicit than any I would have expected to read. He led me to the story of Peter, one of the twelve disciples, who was passionate to serve

Jesus. He reminded me of the incredible leader that Peter was when Jesus said, "Thou art Peter, and upon this rock I will build my church; and the gates of hell shall not prevail against it" (Matt. 16:18).

He showed me how Peter, who with passionate faith once walked upon the water to meet Jesus, was the same Peter who fell asleep after his Lord instructed him to watch and wait. This man who declared, "Even if all fall away on account of you, I never will" (Matt. 26:33 NIV), was the same man who denied Him three times that very night just hours before His death.

And through His teaching, God taught me that grace is for sinners. It is by His grace that I humbly encourage you to seek something more for yourself and for your marriage. You may very well be in a good place today, but God prepares the heart for *tomorrow*.

Regardless of how long you've been married or how strong your relationship, it's inevitable that you will struggle in some way. Love is a beautiful thing, but it's messy at times. Whether we're dealing with a difficult spouse, financial problems, sickness, aging parents, or death, there will be trials that threaten the bond of our marriages, which is why it's imperative that we are prepared.

I can't imagine where I'd be right now—this very minute—if Michael's heart hadn't been prepared for the mess that I made. When I married him, I planned on spending the rest of my life with this man. I didn't expect that his love for me would bring him to the cross.

That testimony of love powers my desire to be clay in the Potter's hands. By the grace of God I want to be transformed into the wife my husband needs me to be.

Walking together through life—that's a beautiful thing, but it definitely has its moments that are messier than others. It's not a math equation that a routine formula can solve, nor is it straightforward or simple. Marriage can be complicated and frustrating at times—we've all been there—but when we yield our hearts to God, we experience the blessings that obedience brings.

This world is cynical when it comes to marriage, believing most won't last. And those that do last? Well, surely one spouse must be a miserable soul. That's what we tend to see when we look at the standard this world has to offer. God's standard, on the other hand, is rich. He offers abundant life to those who are exercised by faith. Joy and peace are ours for the taking. Jesus assured us, "I am come that they might have life, and that they might have it more abundantly" (John 10:10).

When I started exchanging God's ideas for mine, I realized that a beautiful marriage is not only possible; it's inevitable. That's something to be excited about! That's what this book is about: exchanging God's ideas for ours and tuning out the world so that we might quietly tune in to Him.

Before we dig into the rest of the chapters, I want to ease your mind about something, and I want to be up-front about my purpose in writing this book. I didn't write these words to make you feel guilty or inadequate or give you the idea that you don't measure up. If in the end you *do* feel that way, we've both missed the mark. Matthew wrote that our Savior is "meek and lowly in heart," and His "yoke is easy," and His "burden is light" (11:29–30).

I'm a cracked vessel held together by grace, whose deepest desire is to encourage you in your marriage. I don't have it all figured out, and I doubt that I ever will, but I'm learning to lean on the One who does. I'm learning that when I follow His wisdom in lieu of my own, I'm walking in peace, and that peace floods into my marriage.

Before writing this book, I sat down and considered the ways that I wanted to encourage you in your marriage and the areas in which I wanted to challenge you. I made a list of the areas that were dear to my heart and those that I deemed important to being a God-fearing wife. Before long, my thoughts turned to prayer. Will you pray with me?

Dear heavenly Father,

I bring my marriage before You and humbly place it at the foot of Your throne. I know, Lord, that

You are able to do immeasurably more than I could ever do on my own.

Please prepare my heart, teaching me to walk in compassion and grace and to be patient and kind when the going gets tough. Teach me to walk in humility, giving up my right to be right.

Help me to look for the best and to hope for the best in my husband, that I might appreciate him for who he truly is.

Grant me the strength to step back while I allow him to lead. And may this covenant we share be a testimony to others that brings nothing less than glory and honor to You.

Lord, I know that there will be days when we fight; days when we are angry, frustrated, and hurt. I ask that You teach us to handle our conflict wisely.

Please show us how to communicate with loving respect and to read each other's heart. Teach me to be gentle and patient with him.

Equip me to be the wife my husband needs me to be. A woman who is ready to stand beside him in battle and pick him up if he should fall. May You guide my steps and lead me according to Your will, that I might live according to Your purpose.

Father, I ask that You guide us as we seek to express our affection in ways that are pleasing to You. That we won't take each other for granted or lose sight of our joy.

Gently remind us to seize the day and capture the joy of each moment, giving thanks for the big and the small.

Teach me how to be a good friend, and help each of us build a strong friendship.

And finally, may I learn to be content with this life that I'm given as I walk in virtue according to wisdom.

In Jesus' precious name I pray and will continue to pray for my marriage.

Amen.

| TWO |

Walk in Compassion and Grace

WITH CANS IN HAND I FIT THE LAST OF the groceries into what we referred to as our pantry. It was a section of shelving off the kitchen that was intended for food storage, but when you live in a 750-square-foot home with a busy toddler and an in-house book bindery, the pantry is home to everything from diapers to office supplies.

This narrow nook was originally our kitchen. That was all we had when we moved into the little house at the end of the street—a kitchen no bigger than four by eight feet—complete with a single stainless-steel sink, a short countertop, and one small row of cupboards. It was a tight space, but I didn't mind too much because this tiny kitchen was home. It was one little corner of the world that I could call mine.

The term *galley kitchen* may sound glamorous to some, but let me assure you that it wasn't. The cupboards were yellow, the walls were yellow, the ceiling was yellow, and the once-white curtains were yellow. The tile floor? Yellow.

There was no triangle to be found in this kitchen. It was more like an obstacle course in which the fridge and the stove were in a separate room. It's no wonder I was in good shape back then. Making a meal was like running a triathlon with a baby in tow. Run I did, and I enjoyed every minute of it! I probably baked more buns in that house than the Pillsbury Doughboy has seen in a lifetime.

Nothing about that house was pretty, not the commercial gray carpet and not the white paint that covered every wall outside the pantry. It wasn't big or beautiful; it was simply *enough*.

We had a claw-foot tub in the bathroom, which some people thought was nifty, but showers were out of the question for us. So was storage. Our two closets were so tiny that we could not fit a hanger in either of them, so we hung our clothes at an angle. Towels and sheets were stored in baskets, and canned food was often piled on top of the fridge.

Curb appeal was nonexistent. Our back door was the least attractive thing about the house and the very thing that stood out the most. It was a wooden interior door, perhaps taken from the galley kitchen. This worn-out door stood about three feet away from the public sidewalk—an eyesore to anyone who walked by the house. But by the time we were finished setting up house, several people asked if we had hired an interior decorator, and others offered to buy it from us.

The gray carpeting was torn out, and the hardwood floors were refinished. The dining area was transformed into a kitchen with teal-colored walls and black-and-white-checkered flooring. We installed new cupboards and a countertop with a double porcelain sink. I finally got my triangle.

We purchased one of those vintage-style chrome kitchen tables, and Michael refinished the chairs in cherry-colored leather. It was always my dream to have a kitchen that felt like a soda pop shop, and this one definitely did.

I picked up a wallpaper border that was painted with vintage seed packets. It was blue and green, the perfect accent for the teal-colored walls. The harvest gold appliances found their way out the door, while white appliances made their way in. I'm not a huge fan of lace, but when I came across a bolt of tea-stained fabric that was stitched into the pattern of cows, I couldn't resist picking up a few yards to make no-sew café curtains.

I loved to watch Michael as he worked on our home and to help him with things that I could. Truth be told, I'm not the best carpenter, but I can refill a cup of coffee like there's no tomorrow. Together we insulated the back porch and installed a beautiful window that faced our postage-stamp yard. A brand-new steel door complete with a window protected us from the elements of winter. For about forty dollars, I painted the back door a glossy, bright shade of yellow, and later we painted the exterior of the house brick red with hunter-green trim.

When I wasn't with my best friend, Cello, I spent my afternoons hanging wallpaper, painting walls, sewing quilts, and playing with Brendan. There were few things I enjoyed as much as caring for my family and our little red house on the corner.

I'd love to say that those were the best years of our lives because in so many ways they were. Sure Brendan was colicky, which made for sleepless nights and tired mornings, but the time we had together was nothing less than incredible. We went to drive-in movies, took Brendan to swim at the park, danced to songs from the 1980s, and played Monopoly at the kitchen table. I was more in love than I had ever been, and I was happy just being a wife and a mom. Those were the days when our love was beautiful. The days *before* things got messy.

Life has a way of throwing you curveballs when you least expect them, and since I'm not great at baseball, I didn't see this one coming. I don't think my husband did either; we were just two young people in love with big dreams for the future.

Michael had been working for several years at a book bindery when things finally came to a screeching halt. It was closing its doors, which gave him only two options: pick up the pieces of this broken company or look for another job.

After taking it to prayer Michael felt that it was in our best interest to purchase the company. He said that as long as God was opening a door for him, he was ready to walk through it.

I was more of a doubting Thomas, wondering how any of this could possibly be good. We barely had enough money left to buy diapers, never mind purchasing a company, paying a lease on a building, and hiring employees. Michael's answer was that if God was calling him to it, He would also provide a way.

Little did either of us know that our lives were about to go through the fire. You know the refiner's fire that sounds so beautiful when you sing about it? That stuff burns, let me tell you! Imagine walking on hot coals in your bare feet with a one-hundred-pound weight on your shoulders. Make it two.

In our seventh year of marriage, Michael's company, along with three of its employees, crammed their stuff into our little red house on the corner. The basement stairs were temporarily removed, and a hoist was put in to lower heavy equipment. The back room looking out into the yard became an office space, and my beautiful kitchen with the white porcelain sink doubled as a staff room. Two large tables were jammed into the living room where hundreds of books were stacked and ready for binding. The air was filled with dust; the hardwood floors covered in paper. Customers came and went with their books, couriers walked in without knocking, employees sat at my kitchen table to eat, and I silently wept.

I'll never forget the morning when I discovered that Brendan had chicken pox. Wrapped in a blanket and covered in spots, he sat on the couch in the midst of a factory. More than anything I wanted to take back his home and be the mom I once was. I wanted to serve him chicken soup on the couch and cuddle up under a blanket in the privacy of what *used* to be home. I wanted to clean up the mess our lives had become, but to tell you the truth, I felt hopeless. I had started feeling more like an employee than a wife, and I felt our friendship crumble away under the weight of this newfound world we had built for ourselves.

Most of us have good intentions. But while we desire to love people the way that they *should* be loved, our flesh tends to get in the way. When I say flesh, I'm talking about every weakness that contradicts love: being impatient, jealous, unkind, proud, selfish, or arrogant; demanding your own way; and getting angry when others don't love you the way that you think you should be loved. My flesh was definitely in the way, and it was clouding the way I looked at my husband.

The pressure of providing for his family and his struggle to do so were taking a toll on our lives.

Looking back on it now, I can see what I didn't see then: his intentions were incredibly noble. Not only was he seeking a way to provide for his family; he was walking in obedience to God.

I couldn't see that, nor did I want to. All I could see was that my hardwood floors were covered in paper scraps, my walls were scuffed, and my kitchen floor had a gouge in it the size of the Grand Canyon. My husband was my boss, and I was his disgruntled employee.

I loved him, but that loving feeling was wearing dangerously thin. Over the years I've come to learn that a loving feeling is just that, a feeling. It comes as quickly as a gust of wind and can leave just as rapidly. If we want that loving feeling to thrive in marriage, we have to roll up our sleeves and get tough when the going gets rough.

True love, the way God intended it to be, is more than a feeling and much more than two words. It's holding hands as you walk through the fire. It's being patient and kind when everything inside you tells you that this man deserves the wrath of your anger. It's offering grace and forgiveness in the face of despair. It is easier to say and easier to write than it is to live, but as Mom always said, "The best things in life don't come easy."

The best things in life get messy before they get good. God has never promised us days without pain because He knows that trials are the very things that strengthen us and that His grace is made perfect when we are weak. A wise woman knows that joy and peace come from the Lord, while a foolish one seeks happiness anywhere she can find it.

The marks on the floor, the dust in the air, the piles of books that clouded the view of my husband—none of those things were the root of my problem. They were nothing more than trials that tested my faith. My problem was a heart issue that could be healed only by compassion and grace. If I had known that, I would have chosen a different path for my marriage, but instead I chose to let my anger and unforgiveness draw me away and consume my heart with lust. Here's the thing: *love doesn't get angry when others do it wrong.* And we will do it wrong again and again.

Couples in love do a lot of things right, but let's face it, we also tend to do a lot of things wrong. Maybe they aren't even wrong sometimes; they just aren't the way that we'd choose to do them. And so those little things—his leaving dirty socks on the couch or dragging sawdust into the house—can chip away at our patience day after day until we're so angry that we don't remember why.

The path to separation is paved by selfish ambition and pride, but when we move pride aside to make room for love as God designed it to be, we see two hearts joining together as one. His desire for us is that we might be *one* in the bond of unity in the same way that we are one in the union and fellowship of Christ. This is why "the two shall become one flesh" (Mark 10:8 NKJV).

If we want marriage to reflect the relationship between Jesus Christ and His church, and if we want to live in unity, we must be filled with compassion, mercy, and grace. We've been forgiven. Therefore, we have much to forgive, including someone who doesn't love us the way that we think we should be loved. Paul urged us, "Put on then, as God's chosen ones, holy and beloved, compassionate hearts, kindness, humility, meekness, and patience, bearing with one another and, if one has a complaint against another, forgiving each other; as the Lord has forgiven you, so you also must forgive" (Col. 3:12–13 ESV).

Regardless of where you are in your marriage, whether you are dealing with the messy or enjoying your first steps together as husband and wife, be reminded that both of you are on the same team. It's not flesh and blood that you wrestle against as you walk through the fire. There's a spiritual battle that will threaten to tear you apart. Remember that "the trial of your faith, being much more precious than of gold that perisheth, though it be tried with fire, might be found unto praise and honour and glory at the appearing of Jesus Christ" (1 Peter 1:7).

THE CHALLENGE

Although your goal might be to work on your marriage, love must start with the preparation of a graceful heart. Take time out of your day to specifically ask God to lead you in wisdom and teach you to walk in compassion.

Take every opportunity to understand the heart of your husband, and start looking at him in the light of God's glorious grace.

| THREE |

Be Patient and Kind When the Going Gets Tough

ONCE MICHAEL WAS ABLE TO SETTLE HIS business into a shop downtown, the dynamics of our family changed. Five miscarriages and three births later, we went from a family of three to a family of six. I was a stay-at-home mom taking care of the kids, and he was off to work every morning, briefcase in hand.

For the first few weeks, I enjoyed the separation of home and work. Things finally seemed to be falling into place for us. I was ready to settle into a normal life when I realized that things weren't normal at all. Michael was working far more hours than I wanted him to.

He woke up about five o'clock every morning. After he read the Bible, showered, and had breakfast, he was off to work with our only car, not to return until around nine or ten at night. Some days he'd get off work early to spend an evening with us. But by then he was so exhausted that he couldn't stand on his feet.

His work schedule was Sunday to Thursday. On Fridays and Saturdays he was supposed to be off so he could be with the family, but unfortunately, so many of those days he had to go to work because machines were down or staff didn't show up. Long days took their toll on him, and his face showed it.

I could go on and on complaining about how Michael wasn't there for me during that season of our life together. If I gave him the podium, he could certainly think of a few things to say about me, but he wouldn't. He's gracious that way.

Going on and on about his faults wouldn't serve any purpose, but that's what I did. I took count of his faults and kept track of each one. I had forgotten what 1 Corinthians says about love: "It is not rude, it is not self-seeking, it is not easily angered, it keeps no record of wrongs" (13:5 NIV).

Record keeping damages our hearts and feeds the root of bitterness within us, while love heals the wound. When we love someone we "beareth all things, believeth all things, hopeth all things, endureth all things" (1 Cor. 13:7). In other words, when we love someone, we believe in him. We look past the messy to find the misunderstood intentions inside him.

During this difficult time the piano came into our lives. Our children were still quite young, and like most parents, we thought that music might do them some good. If they were going to be anything like my husband, they'd be playing in no time.

We started talking about it. Mostly we talked about the fact that we couldn't afford anything bigger than a toddler's toy—not unless we lived on bread and bologna for the next year. As much as I like bologna, we decided to wait on the Lord for supply.

The funny thing with supply is that God doesn't always meet our level of expectation, does He? Sometimes it's a no, and other times He'll exceed it beyond anything we could have imagined for ourselves. But one thing I know for sure: He always has our best interest at heart.

When my sister told me that a friend was giving away the family's upright piano, I was eager to take a look at it. But free wasn't all that appealing when I saw its condition. The paint job—if you could call it that—was a thick layer of black-brown with extra-large splotches of who knows what here and there. Not to mention that it was terribly out of tune. I had expected to see something more along the lines of the handsome piano with which I grew up. In any event we thanked her friend with a smile, and three hours later my husband and a few strong men hauled it into our living room, where they placed it across from the sofa.

It sat there, virtually untouched, until I was ready to take it on. I don't know what drove me to do it, but one spring morning I woke up, took one look at the dark stain, and decided to refinish the wood. I had taken on small projects before, but nothing of this magnitude. I figured it couldn't possibly look any worse. I got to work, stripping and sanding layer after layer until I discovered its worth hidden beneath years of neglect. To my surprise, it was nothing less than a vintage, burled-walnut piano. With each stroke of my hand, it returned to the beautiful piece it once was.

God could have sent us a brand-spanking-new keyboard with all the bells and whistles, but rather than send us easy, He gave us a treasure complete with life lessons that taught us the value of hard work. Looking back on it now, I can say, "I get it, Lord. I understand the parable of the piano You gave us and how it relates to our marriage." Neglecting to care for each other more than we cared for ourselves, wanting to take more from our marriage than we were ready to give, and failing to lean on God's wisdom more than our own were the layers of filth and stain that built up over time. One by one, each piled up on the other, concealing the beauty and depth of our covenant. It was unrecognizable, not to mention the fact that we were out of tune with each other. That is until that day when love found me in the darkness and carried me back to the light. I realized what a mess I had made of things and the role that sin had played in my life. Until then my primary concern was pleasing myself and getting what I wanted from this marriage. The more I focused inward, the less I focused on the Lord.

The minute we allow ourselves to be drawn away by our lust, whether it's a baby step or a giant step toward sin, we expose ourselves to Satan, who is ready and willing to deceive us into believing that we can and should step farther yet. I was standing in a pit of sin and shame, but Michael loved me enough to show me that marriage God's way is worth fighting for. That's the day I woke up and got to work restoring our marriage and redeeming the love we once had.

We both needed to be rescued that day. We had failed each other, but more important we had failed the One we loved the most—our Savior. If we wanted this marriage to flourish, first and foremost we needed a Christ-centered relationship. We needed to reflect His love to each other.

Once we started loving and respecting each other from a place of humility, we began to see the beauty of new life emerge. With each step of forgiveness, understanding, communication, and grace, it's being restored to the beautiful love it once was.

If we could take back the past, we would. Knowing what we know now, we'd do so many things differently than we did. We'd handle each other with care. We'd give more than we get. We'd listen more than we speak.

Being patient and kind through hard times isn't the easiest thing to do. Love can be confusing and gut-wrenching. There will be seasons of our lives that are so awesome we wonder how life can be so incredibly good, and there will be other seasons that bring us to our knees in prayer. Those are the ones when we need each other the most.

Here's a letter I received from a reader who was feeling the sting of a new season. This one was leaving her feeling rejected and tense. We all go through difficult times, but the important thing to remember is that the way we choose to handle disappointment sets the stage for our future.

Dear Darlene,

I'm not sure what to do. I understand that I need to respect and submit to my husband but lately it's been difficult to do so.

He recently changed jobs and ever since the transition he's been out of sorts. Normally he's in a good mood when he comes home, but not so much lately. He's been grumpy and tense. And yes, I've tried to talk to him about it, but we always seem to end up arguing and we're right back to square one.

I know he realizes it, too, because he apologizes often, but then he'll come home from work and be just as grumpy as he was the night before. He's a Christian, so he's not abusive, but he's easily frustrated and cranky.

I don't want an apology as much as I want my old husband back, but I feel like I'm losing a part of him, and I'm worried that I won't get it back.

We used to work out our problems together, but now he's keeping things to himself and it hurts me. I feel like he's turning his back on me.

Some days I wonder why I bother trying because I feel like he's giving up.

Do you have any advice?

Feeling Left Out

Dear Feeling Left Out,

As I'm reading your thoughts, a few things come to mind . . .

The first is that of intentions. It sounds to me like your husband has good intentions. Obviously he does because he apologizes to you often. But like all of us he's struggling with the flesh. By that I mean that he's giving in to stress or anger. It could be any number of reasons—like being so tired at the end of the day or dealing with things that stress him out.

The fact that he's just stepped into a new job is

probably affecting his mood more than you imagine. It's hard not to take it personally, which is why you'll have to exercise patience and understanding during this time.

Consider what Paul said about his struggle with the flesh: "I know that good itself does not dwell in me, that is, in my sinful nature. For I have the desire to do what is good, but I cannot carry it out. For I do not do the good I want to do, but the evil I do not want to do—this I keep on doing" (Rom. 7:18–19 NIV). We all struggle with the flesh in one way or another regardless of our good intentions. As a result we let ourselves and others down.

The second thing is that couples often get caught up in a cycle where they give only as much as they get. In other words, if you start feeling that you're not being loved enough, your knee-jerk reaction is to mirror that behavior, and you start asking yourself, *Why should I love someone who could care less about my feelings?* And so you start to love him less, respect him less, and admire him less. The result is that a man comes home from work to a frustrated wife who doesn't admire or respect him as much as she used to, and he reacts to her behavior, which keeps the cycle going. The way to change it is to give more than you get.

In God's Word we discover that love is sacrificial. It gives when the going gets tough. It gives when it doesn't get.

How's that fair? What if it isn't going both ways? I got to thinking about that one day when this verse came to mind: "Without faith it is impossible to please him: for he that cometh to God must believe that he is, and that he is a rewarder of them that diligently seek him" (Heb. 11:6). Don't miss this: He rewards those who earnestly seek Him. As long as we keep our eyes focused on God and understand that He is the One—the only One—we should look to for a reward, a sacrificial life starts to make a lot more sense.

But there's more. If we are told in Scripture that an unbelieving husband can be drawn to the Lord by a faithful wife, we can apply the same principle to that of a believing husband. Our behavior can greatly influence our husbands.

You've done well in communicating your thoughts to him. Continue to communicate with patience and grace; keep on loving and praying and keeping the faith.

I hope I've helped to encourage you.

Blessings,

Darlene

I can't count the number of times that I receive letters and comments from readers who say, "I get what you're saying, but let's not forget that love is give-and-take. This has to go both ways."

The way of the Lord is uncommon to man, and the way that He loves is amazing. Those who follow His lead seek to love as *He* loves. We don't give because we are given. We give because it's the way of the Lord. We serve a God who makes the sun to rise on both the good and the evil and the rain to fall on the just and the unjust (Matt. 5:45). He loved us while we were yet sinners, giving His Son to die for our sins.

Jesus said, "If ye love them which love you, what thank have ye? for sinners also love those that love them. And if ye do good to them which do good to you, what thank have ye? for sinners also do even the same. And if ye lend to them of whom ye hope to receive, what thank have ye? for sinners also lend to sinners, to receive as much again" (Luke 6:32–34). Jesus is telling us that we must stop the cycle of give-and-take by going the extra mile. He is calling us to love the unlovable and to give more than we get. That includes giving love and respect.

After Jesus broke bread with the twelve disciples, we're told that He rose from the table and girded Himself as a servant. He then proceeded to wash the feet of His disciples. In those days it was a servant's job to do that. People didn't have the luxury of paved roads or walking paths as we do. Their sandaled feet were exposed to dust and dirt, so washing them for someone else was considered a dirty job. It called for humility.

Why did He do it? Why would the King of all kings take on the role of a servant? For the same reason that Jesus did anything—to fulfill the will of the Father. If His motivation was to gain the favor of His disciples, He would have been sorely disappointed when one of the twelve sold Him for thirty pieces of silver that very night or when another denied Him three times. His actions were a display of *unselfish love*.

> In the same manner we are to love people, not because they *deserve* it but because it is the will of our Father in heaven. Mother Teresa said, "There is always the danger that we may . . . just do the work for the sake of the work. . . . This is where the respect and the love and the devotion come in—that we give it and we do it to God, to Christ, and that's why we try to do it as beautifully as possible."[1]

God's will is that we freely give of ourselves to the other. When we put that plan in action, we create an atmosphere of love and respect, but the minute we start to reverse it, the atmosphere changes. If I had stopped for a minute to do that, if my love wasn't as self-seeking as it was, or if I had believed in my husband enough to give him the benefit of the doubt, I would have seen a man who was doing everything he understood to be good and to supply for his family. If I wasn't blinded by anger, I might have understood the sacrifices he made for us.

Once you look past the mess of human frailty and error, you see that love is a beautiful thing.

THE CHALLENGE

When you and your husband are going through tough times, make an extra effort to encourage him. Also be intentional about turning your eyes from your problems and onto the Lord. Seek Him for your reward, and you will find it.

FOUR

Give Up Your Right to Be Right

IT WASN'T YOUR USUAL SATURDAY AFTER-
noon.

We had a lot of talking to do. Money talk. You know—the uncomfortable, I-want-to-avoid-this-topic discussion, where we chat about our finances to see where our money's being spent. We desperately try to avoid pointing fingers, but the temptation is strong nonetheless.

Michael likes to spend on gifts. Whatever the occasion, I can be sure that my husband won't show up empty-handed. At Christmastime our tree is surrounded by presents, and a birthday is a weeklong celebration. Buying gifts for his family is one of Michael's greatest pleasures, but it's also a topic of contention for us. And yes, he gives to others, too—nonstop.

I like buying gifts for people, but not anywhere near to the extent that he does. Just a few weeks ago I had a birthday. He bought me new cushions for our garden furniture, a large cooking pot, a set of cutlery, a spoon rest, a napkin holder, a framed print, and a purebred Pug puppy. It's nice to get gifts but overwhelming sometimes.

I'm more of a small spender, but I like to spend often. I want to be able to go out on dates with him, take the kids out for ice cream, pick up some cute shoes, and buy clothes when we need them. I'm a spend-as-you-go kind of girl, while Michael's a spend-all-at-once kind of guy. In other words, we have different opinions when it comes to our finances.

And so we sat down. With a laptop in front of us, we went over our spending and took a look at our income to determine the outcome. Why were we over budget? Where should we cut back? What were our biggest concerns?

After about two hours of talking and searching and making notes, I started getting tense. I couldn't help feeling that Michael was painting me into a corner. All the things that he wanted to cut out of our budget were the things that I enjoy most. I didn't want to get angry, and I didn't want to point fingers, but I found myself doing both.

I'd start, and I'd stop. And then I'd do it all over again. "Maybe we should talk about all the Christmas gifts *you* bought last December," I said. "And look at November. How many times did you go to the mall?"

I wasn't happy about the conversation, and I certainly wasn't happy about the way I was handling things. I was trying to be kind and considerate, but my anger kept rearing its head.

"Okay," he said in the most considerate way, "but can we talk about this without pointing fingers? There are a lot of things that I need to change."

Then I saw something happen that I've never seen before, at least not in the physical sense. Michael's flesh was at war with his spirit, and his spirit was winning the battle. I could tell that he was ready to walk out of the room and slam the door behind him. He stood up for a second before sitting back down at least once or twice. Every time he resisted the urge to give up and walk out, he chose to be patient and kind. I could tell just by watching Michael that there was an internal struggle inside him. He was sacrificing his emotional turmoil for the good of our marriage. It was more important for him to walk in peace than it was to *win*. His loving-kindness is a constant reminder of how it's better to *do right* than it is to *be right*.

Watching him fight for our marriage reminds me that sacrificial love is so important to achieving unity. That's what marriage is about, really—it's growing together as one so that we reflect the unity of the covenant between Jesus Christ and the church. Paul wrote, "God, who is rich in mercy, for his great love wherewith he loved us, even when we were dead in sins, hath quickened us together with Christ, (by grace ye are saved)" (Eph. 2:4–5). Paul talked about the same kind of love—*agape* love—in his letter to the Corinthians, instructing them to be patient, kind, considerate, and humble. It's also the same love described here: "Greater love hath no man than this, that a man lay down his life for his friends" (John 15:13).

We might never be called to *physically* lay down our lives for the sake of a friend. I know that I never have. But time and again we are called to lay down our lives in a *spiritual* sense. We're called to walk humbly through this world, esteeming others higher than ourselves.

An incredibly interesting passage of Scripture appears in John 21. I love to read from the Greek translation whenever I can because things just pop off the page and speak to me. It was the third time that Jesus appeared to His disciples after His resurrection. He was speaking to Peter: "Simon, son of Jonas, lovest [*agape*] thou me more than these? He saith unto him, Yea, Lord; thou knowest that I love [*phileo*] thee. He saith unto him, Feed my lambs" (John 21:15).

Let me point out a contrast here. *Agape* is a *sacrificial* love while *phileo* is a *brotherly/friendship* love. We'll talk more about the love of friendship in another chapter, but in this one I want to specifically focus on *agape* love. This love calls us to give our lives for others.

That was Peter's mind-set when he said, "Lord, why cannot I follow thee now? I will lay down my life for thy sake"

(John 13:37). Peter expressed incredible devotion, which for the most part was characteristic of him. But here we see a different Peter: "He saith to him again the second time, Simon, son of Jonas, lovest [*agape*] thou me? He saith unto him, Yea, Lord; thou knowest that I love [*phileo*] thee. He saith unto him, Feed my sheep" (John 21:16). Peter didn't say, "Yes, Lord, I *agape* you," as we expect him to say, because he was walking in *humility*.

If you remember, in the first chapter I said, "Peter, who with passionate faith once walked upon the water to meet Jesus, was the same Peter who fell asleep after his Lord had instructed him to watch and wait. This man who declared, 'Even if all fall away on account of you, I never will' (Matt. 26:33 NLT), was the same man who denied Him three times that very night just hours before His death."

What we see here is Peter's transformation of faith. Peter knew that he was weak and that he had failed his Lord when he denied Him three times just hours before His death. Jesus understood his struggle in the flesh and said "unto him the third time, Simon, son of Jonas, lovest [*phileo*] thou me? Peter was grieved because he said unto him the third time, Lovest [*phileo*] thou me? And he said unto him, Lord, thou knowest all things; thou knowest that I love [*phileo*] thee. Jesus saith unto him, Feed my sheep" (John 21:17).

Peter was grieved because he desperately wanted to say, "Yes, Lord, I *agape* You." He wanted to be the man that he *knew* he should be. He wanted to lay down his life for his Lord, but he knew that he was a sinner growing in grace.

Jesus offered him grace when He asked, "Will you love [*phileo*] Me?" In essence He was saying, "This is what I ask, this is what I hope for, but this is what I know you can give Me."

We're all like Peter in that we're growing in grace. And as He did with Peter, God is calling us to love with a sacrificial love.

Jesus said that all the commandments can be summed up in these two: "Thou shalt love the Lord thy God with all thy heart, and with all thy soul, and with all thy mind. . . . And the second is like unto it, Thou shalt love thy neighbour as thyself" (Matt. 22:37, 39). Do you wonder what kind of love Jesus was talking about? You guessed it—*agape* love.

Loving my husband is more than just having the warmies for him. If I love him, I must be willing to walk in humility for the good of our marriage. Laying down my life for Michael is an act of laying down my selfishness, anger, and pride. It's never an easy thing to do, but it's the most Christ-centered way I can live. No, I'm not there yet, but I'm learning and growing in grace.

I'm committed to living out my vows and reflecting the covenant of my Lord; therefore, I must be willing to go the extra mile when it is required of me.

When my flesh is at war with my spirit, I have a choice. I can either let my flesh win or I can exercise virtue. I can fly off the handle, or I can patiently offer him kindness. I've come to learn that choosing the right path is well worth the effort.

Love is so many things, but the heart of the matter is that beautiful love is Christ-centered.

Love Is Patient

Being married to someone who is gentle and kind is easy, but being married to someone who frustrates you requires patience and sacrifice on your part.

Peter addressed this very issue, whether it's in the home or the workplace, saying that it is commendable when we bear suffering for the sake of our faith. Why? Because true love is not only patient and kind; it doesn't get angry when others do it wrong. It bears all things, always hopes, and always perseveres.

Love Is Kind

You might very well pass as being kind to your husband, but I wonder how many of us go out of our way to do so. When Michael and I were dating, we made every effort to be kind to each other. We smiled, we hugged, we phoned each other, and we bought each other little gifts. I still have some of the letters and cards that we exchanged in those days. It's beautiful to look back on our love notes and remember the excitement they brought us.

Making a kind first impression is a great way to impress the man you love, but when you continue the kindness long after you're married, you leave a lasting impression on him.

Love Does Not Envy

I used to wonder how love could possibly envy. When I was dating Michael, I could envy the women he talked about, sure, but envy him? Never. At least I didn't think I ever would—until we got married and he became the head of the house.

Living in submission to my husband and allowing him to lead our family have benefits, the most important being that we are living in obedience to God. But with that said, there are days when I consider his role in our marriage, and envy creeps in with its doubt and its questions. *Wouldn't it be nice if I were in charge?*

Those thoughts aren't rooted in the will of God; they stem from selfish ambition and pride. Loving God means that I will love His commandments, and loving my husband means that I must allow him to live out his God-given role. It's not always easy, but that's what sacrificial love calls us to do.

Love Does Not Boast

There can be a fine line between boasting and sharing good news. Whenever something great happens in my life, my first thoughts are to thank God for His goodness and then call Michael at work.

I think those are the best kinds of phone calls, don't you? I love it when Michael calls me to tell me about something awesome, and I've never really thought of that as boasting.

We can be guilty of boasting, however, when we start keeping track of who did what and how much. Say, for example, that Michael has been out enjoying a day taking photos while I've been at home doing laundry. Boasting about how much I got done and how busy I was isn't the most loving thing to do. Sure I want him to notice, and he will in his time. But the loving thing to do would be to ask him about his day and take pleasure in *him*.

We can also be guilty of boasting when we start comparing ourselves to our spouses. Saying, "Wow, I ran five miles this morning, and I feel great!" can be good, but if we follow it up by saying something like, "When was the last time you got off the couch and exercised?" it's not so good, is it?

Love Is Not Proud

In understanding this facet of love, you can think of it this way: when you love someone, you are willing to walk in humility, esteeming others higher than yourself. All Christians are commanded to live this way.

Those who walk in humility are able to resolve conflict more quickly because they aren't afraid to apologize first.

They are more concerned about protecting their relationships than they are about protecting their egos.

When you realize that it's more important to win the heart of your husband than it is to win an argument, you're seeing the fruit of mature love.

Love Does Not Dishonor Others

Honor your husband by being his cheerleader and trustworthy companion. This is important to do when you're with him and also when he's out of your sight. If your tongue has been babbling on for several years, consider it a wild horse. You need to tame that horse by training it thought by thought and word by word—taking every thought captive—until you're willing to yield to the obedience of Christ.

You dishonor your husband and hurt him deeply when you say things that you don't mean in the heat of an argument. Letting off steam that way is immature because it means that you're losing control of your emotions. Sacrificial love isn't easy, but it's well worth the effort.

Love Is Not Self-Seeking

Marriage isn't fifty-fifty. Love isn't about taking turns, waiting to be served, or keeping track of who apologized last. Why not? Because true love seeks to please another more than oneself.

When you love someone, you want the best for him, and you hope for the best. Love gives up its right to be *right* and steps down so that the other person can shine.

Without pride we wouldn't need to address this. It wouldn't be an issue in any relationship. Pride causes us to take our eyes off God and move them onto ourselves. But we're called to be Christlike, which means that we love the unlovable and give of ourselves sacrificially.

Love Is Not Easily Angered

Keeping our cool isn't always easy, but every time we let go and let God, we exercise that muscle of self-control. I say "self-control" here because we need to bring our flesh under the subjection of the Spirit. Our flesh wants nothing more than to stamp our feet and have our own way, but the Spirit calls us to be tender-hearted and controlled. That's where our true strength lies.

When the Spirit is in control, we see the fruit of "love, joy, peace, longsuffering, gentleness, [and] goodness" (Gal. 5:22). But when the flesh is out of control, we get angry, short-tempered, abrupt, and stressed out.

Love Keeps No Record of Wrongs

When you really think about what that phrase means— "keeps no record of wrongs"—you realize that this attitude closes the door on resentment. If I were to pinpoint the one thing that led me to almost destroy my marriage, it would be that I was keeping a record of wrongs. And the very thing that transformed my marriage to the place it is now is that Michael *didn't* keep a record of wrongs. While I was at my very worst, he gave me his *best*.

When I hear the constant complaints about who's doing more in a marriage, I can't help feeling that we're placing love on a scale. We're more concerned that it might tip one way or the other than we are about loving in the best way we know how.

Jesus tipped the scales big time. While we were yet sinners—lying, stealing, cheating, self-centered sinners—He gave up His life for us. He took the weight of our sin upon Himself and died in the most horrific way so that we might have life.

Love Does Not Delight in Evil

I don't delight in evil, do I? I don't think that I do, but when I stop to examine the many ways that I am tempted to do so, I think that I may be guilty at times.

When I'm angry, a part of me wants to let go of my anger and get on with my life. But another part of me—the flesh—desires to stew in the anger as long as I can.

Then there's another evil that needs to be brought under control—negativity. My friend says, "Don't invite negative feelings over for dinner, or they'll get fat." I love that thought

because it's one that I can relate to. The more that we enter-
tain negative thoughts, the more likely they are to stick
around for a while.

Love Rejoices with the Truth

Rejoicing in truth is a vital part of loving someone. It's important that we understand what this means, especially if we are
walking in submission to our husbands. We are to obey our
husbands, unless that obedience compromises a biblical truth
or separates us from the Lord.

The apostles were brought before the Sanhedrin and
questioned by the high priest. They had specifically been
instructed not to preach the truth of Jesus Christ. When questioned about their disobedience, Peter and the other apostles
answered and said, "We ought to obey God rather than men"
(Acts 5:29). So we are to obey those in authority, including
our husbands, but our allegiance must always be to God first.

Love Always Protects

A wife is to protect her husband's reputation by speaking
highly of him to others. She is also wise to protect him by cov-
ering him in prayer.

Prayer is a powerful tool in any marriage, but too often it's
considered a last resort. We are to pray without ceasing, but

that doesn't mean we'll be in the prayer closet 24/7. Praying can be as simple as talking to God while folding laundry, thanking Him while out for a walk, or offering thanks while holding hands around the dinner table. Our husbands need extra protection when they are out in the world.

Love Always Trusts

I can trust Michael more than anyone else. After twenty-five years, I've come to know him as a man of integrity—one who walks the talk. He's not a liar, a cheater, a gambler, or a drunk. Praise God!

But I'm still learning to trust his intentions. The other day, for example, I had a lot of driving to do and a lot of writing to do, and we had just gotten a new puppy. It was such a crazy day. I felt that every minute I wasn't driving, I was potty training a pup.

Around three o'clock Michael called to tell me that he had to work late. I know he's a busy man, but I couldn't help wondering whether he was dodging us to get out of driving the kids here and there and potty training the pup.

The more I entertained the thought, the more it bothered me until I stopped to realize that I wasn't giving my husband the benefit of the doubt. I was jumping to conclusions instead of taking him at his word.

We can avert a lot of conflict in marriage when we trust

our husbands' intentions. We can avoid a lot of stress, we can temper a lot of anger, and we can eliminate a lot of hurt when we trust them.

Love Always Hopes

Some women reading this book have wonderful marriages, but many of you don't. Frankly, many people are ready to give up on their marriages and walk away. I know this because I hear it said all too often.

When you're the only one who seems to care about your marriage, and you seem to be the only one working on it, you might start to ask yourself, *What's the point?* Before you give up, I want to remind you of something: you serve an unfailing God "who is able to do exceeding abundantly above all" that you ask or think (Eph. 3:20). If you are praying for your marriage, you can be certain that God is at work.

Don't give up hope.

Love Always Perseveres

Remove the idea of divorce from your mind. Determine to work with your husband until you find a solution rather than walk away when the going gets tough. Leaving that door open is only setting yourself up for a failure.

Marriage is a covenant that reflects the union between

Jesus Christ and the church. We have the assurance that He won't turn His back on us. His grace and forgiveness are unfailing, which is the same mind-set that we should have toward others. We've been forgiven much; therefore, we have much to forgive.

Before I move on, I know that you might be reading this and thinking, *Stick around when the going gets tough? Isn't that encouraging domestic abuse?* Let me be clear: there's a difference between a husband who is grumpy and one who is habitually abusive. And we all know that there are times when it's vital to remove oneself and one's children from an abusive situation.

When we walk in obedience, we're trusting God with an unknown future by placing our hearts in His hands. It's not easy to do because we think we know exactly what will make us happy, and we're determined to get there. God will lead us to a much better place according to His incomparable wisdom.

One day I want to be able to stand before my Savior and say, "Yes, Lord. I walked in obedience, and I trusted You with my life." Thus far I've failed on many accounts, but I'm learning to loosen my grip.

Love Never Fails

One thing I know about marriage is this: while the journey leads you through the most breathtaking experience of your life, the road is paved with many obstacles. There are things in this world designed to tear us apart, and there always will be as long as Satan is roaming this earth. But couples who face the obstacles together and handle each hurdle in faith are the ones who reap the benefits brought by obedience.

God doesn't give up on you. Don't give up on your marriage. Sacrificial love is what the best marriages are made of.

We stepped into our marriage with the commitment to love, honor, and cherish each other until death. Like Peter, I was ready and willing to lay down my life for this man at the drop of a hat. But as the years went by and the hats started dropping, I realized that *agape* love was more of a challenge than I ever dreamed it would be. When push came to shove, I found myself standing against enemy lines in a battle against the flesh, and I was losing the war.

Peter's testimony of faith is a reminder that we all must stand guard lest we are tempted and fall: "Be sober, be vigilant; because your adversary the devil, as a roaring lion, walketh about, seeking whom he may devour" (1 Peter 5:8). Satan is wily, wise, and wicked. He seeks to destroy marriage because he knows that the marriage covenant is ordained by God.

If you want to stand strong in the faith, you have to start by planting your feet firmly in Christ. Get into the Word, get into prayer, and most important, get into a right relationship with the Father. When God is for you, nothing can stand against you. The victory is His. Hallelujah!

THE CHALLENGE

None of us can say that we have it all together when it comes to loving each other. As much as we might desire to love well, we all struggle against the flesh.

And so my challenge to you is to practice. Get used to holding your tongue, exercise patience, and train yourself to walk in humility. And take this to prayer before you start fighting the flesh on your own.

FIVE

Appreciate Him for Who He Truly Is

BY THE TIME I HIT SEVENTH GRADE I HAD landed myself a sweet job that was the envy of most girls my age. I was the girl who made fuzzy dice. Yes, the same dice that hung in nearly every car across the nation.

It was the 1970s when Afros were big, the Bee Gees were bigger, and J. R. Ewing was the talk of the town. Some people were buying pet rocks, while others were busy knotting macramé owls, belts, and plant hangers. Eight-tracks were hip, but nothing was quite as hip as *The Brady Bunch* and its very own Greg, except maybe a pair of red fuzzy dice.

Each evening I'd cut, stuff, and stitch my way to another paycheck from the comfort of home. With nothing more than a 1954 Singer Featherweight, I produced one pair after another. It gave me three options: forward, backward, and zig-zag. What more could I possibly need?

I loved that little machine, and I wasn't about to part ways with it anytime soon. It was my little hummer, and we got along well enough to earn me enough money for more fabric and a few more patterns. After all, that was the goal. By ninth grade, I was skilled in my trade, sewing myself at least one new outfit a week—two if I could!

Not only was I the girl who could sew; I was also the girl who had her own fabric store—if you could call it that. We did.

My uncle owned a fabric shop, and while he was in transition of moving it from one town to the next, the supplies were stored in our basement. All of them! We had cutting tables, bolts of fabric, sewing notions, and patterns. Basically, we had everything that his fabric store had, except it was in the basement.

And it gets better. I was given permission to use any and all of the fabric I wanted.

Mom said, "If you want to sew yourself clothing, then you can use whatever you like."

I had a little piece of heaven all to myself. Every evening I'd make my way down to the basement where I'd spend hours on end looking at patterns and searching through fabric. It was incredibly peaceful and almost surreal. Not many people get to be immersed in their hobby quite like I did. With endless possibilities at my disposal, my only dilemma was deciding what to make first.

Why am I talking about fabric? These woven pieces of cloth resemble people in so many ways. Our precious moments, our ups, and our downs have been sewn together by countless threads forming characteristics that make us unique.

Time has taught me that people are just as different from each other as one fabric is from another. The days, the hours, and the minutes of our lives have been woven together in their own way. This process of knitting and weaving started before we were born and will continue throughout our lives. The psalmist summed it up: "You created my inmost being; you knit me together in my mother's womb" (Ps. 139:13 NIV).

We all know that we were created differently and that we've lived differently, and yet we tend to hold on to these ideals of what the perfect husband should look like, comparing one to the other. Comparison can be a slippery slope that leads to envy and strife. It's also something that tends to grow if left unchecked.

Have you ever gone shopping for off-white paint? I have a few times, and it certainly messed with my eyes. The chips looked the same until I held them up against a pure white sample. That's when I saw the differences between eggshell, seashell, and bird shell and realized that not one of them is pure white. A few years ago we went home with several gallons of white paint only to later discover that it was light purple. Yuck. Our master bedroom was mauve, and we were not happy campers. When we start comparing our husbands to what we view as perfection, it's like we're holding them up against a white paint chip. We begin to notice their flaws, and the closer we look, the more flaws we see.

Before you begin to compare or if you're already in the process of comparing your husband to others, take a step back and choose a better path that is paved with compassion and grace. In 1 Corinthians 13:7 we're told that love "beareth all things, believeth all things, hopeth all things, endureth all things." Isn't love beautiful? When you truly love someone, you look for the best in him, and you hope for the best. That's when you begin to see him in the light of God's grace.

The world is doing a great job of making your husband feel like a failure already; he doesn't need to hear it from you. What he *does* need to hear is that he is valued, loved, appreciated, and respected for the man that he is.

Our society tends to depict men as lazy, thoughtless slobs. When did this start, and why do we let it continue? I know of so many husbands who are sensitive, caring men, including my own. It's time for this world to stop believing that men can't be anything more than obnoxious, insensitive boys and start looking at them as men who were woven together by the hands of an almighty God, created in *His* image and for *His* pleasure. We have an opportunity to build up our husbands and to support them as they are growing in grace.

Several years ago, a couple came over to our house for the evening. We got to talking about our jobs, and after about five minutes the woman piped up and said to her husband, "Why can't you support your family like Michael does? Why does your wife have to go off to work?"

You could have cut the silence with a knife, but thankfully we didn't have one handy, or he might have used it on her. Their family situation was much different from ours. We're several years older than they are, and they have more children. Not to mention the fact that I'm a writer who *works* from home. She didn't realize that while one husband is denim, the other is knit. No two are the same.

Recently, a reader asked, "How can a woman compliment her husband if all the man does is come home grumpy and mean to his children and wife every day?" She had a good question, and I know that some of you might be thinking the very same thing: *All this advice sounds good in theory, but what about those marriages that are one-sided? Would we be lying if we tell grumpy husbands that they are awesome?*

My answer is that we can find good in anyone if we are willing to look for it. We're talking about human beings who are made in the image of God. And yes, they might be grumpy at times, but if we ever hope to turn that situation around, we must be willing to offer them *grace*. What is grace exactly? It's *undeserved* mercy.

I get letters from men who ask me to pray for their marriages. These men are constantly under pressure. They carry the weight of spiritual leadership on their shoulders, and they're under financial pressure as well. Many are concerned that they could lose their jobs at any moment and then lose their houses and their cars. And what are they craving? A little praise from their wives.

Other men tell me that they can't shake the feeling that they are complete failures. Things could be going well in their businesses. They're at the top of their game, and the future is bright, but a voice inside them whispers, "It's not enough."

Unfortunately, it's not always a whisper, and it's not always inside. Sometimes it's the wife who's gotten so used to nagging that she doesn't realize the message she's sending with each cutting remark.

It breaks my heart when I hear these comments from men. What's making them feel like losers? If we don't remind them that they are winners, who will? Men like affection, men like respect, and men like good food; we all know that. But we tend to forget that they also need encouragement. They need to be reminded that they are incredible men and that we love them unconditionally. When we follow the pattern of marriage as God intended us to, we honor our spouses with our thoughts as well as our words.

All praise to God if you don't compare your husband to others. But if you do, even if it's an unspoken meditation of the heart, carefully consider your thoughts. Could it be that you don't realize the gift that he is? Consider this passage:

> I saw that all toil and all achievement spring from one person's envy of another. This too is meaningless, a chasing after the wind.
>
> Fools fold their hands
> and ruin themselves.
>
> Better one handful with tranquillity
> than two handfuls with toil
> and chasing after the wind. (Eccl. 4:4–6 NIV)

Reading this passage of Scripture, I got to wondering how often I'm chasing the wind. Am I the kind of wife who appreciates Michael, or am I too busy counting the blessings of others to notice my own?

Last month I went to IKEA with a friend, and I picked up a gadget that resembles a towel rack. You fasten it to the kitchen wall and hang cups and utensils on it. I'm sure it would look great in my kitchen if it wasn't still in the package.

Four weekends have passed, and every Saturday I've asked Michael to hang it up for me. I asked him again today, and he said that he left his drill at work so he wouldn't be able to get to it for a few days.

I could do it myself, and if it called for a hammer and a nail I would. But when it comes to fastening screws, I just can't seem to get it quite right. I'm really clumsy, and I suspect that I'd make a mess of the wall. So it waits.

By the fourth weekend, I start thinking about all of my friends with gadgets that their husbands have put together. I start thinking about how pretty their kitchens are and the work that must have gone into making them so.

I open Facebook, and sure enough I see more. One of my friends has posted a photo of the swinging bed that her husband is making for their son—a platform that's suspended from the ceiling by lag bolts and cables. I think about it for a minute and realize that this is the same woman who just had hardwood floors put in her home. She also had the kitchen remodeled along with the cutest pot rack fastened to the ceiling above the new island.

It's hard not to compare myself to them when my thirteen-dollar project is sitting on the counter collecting dust while the rest of the world races past. But the one thing I know about envy is that it takes our eyes away from the blessings at hand.

Would I love my husband any more than I do right now if he hung up that rack today? Or could it be that I'd be too busy thinking about the next project and watching what others are doing to realize the blessing he is?

Just typing that sentence reminds me that he recently finished remodeling a room in the basement, and last summer he built the most incredible wooden sidewalk as well as installed beautiful lights in the backyard. The truth is that I was too focused on the rack to consider it—at least until now.

Jealousy and comparison are dangerous things that can creep up unnoticed in any area of life, including marriage. They bring on stress and a feeling of inadequacy and take our eyes off our Father's will for us. That's why it's so important to always keep them in check.

Today it might be a small thing like a rack in the kitchen, but what will it be tomorrow?

The Lord cautions us: "You shall not covet your neighbor's house. You shall not covet your neighbor's wife, or his male or female servant, his ox or donkey, or anything that belongs to your neighbor" (Ex. 20:17 NIV). We are warned against coveting for a reason. It's sinful, and it's consuming. It's the polar opposite of contentment and leads us to look outside our marriages for happiness.

I know what coveting did to my life, and I see what it did to my heart. But here's the thing that's not talked about enough—it's becoming an epidemic. Social media has opened an all-too-convenient door between the sexes. Flirting has never been easier. It's private, it's convenient, and it's instantly gratifying. All you have to do is open your chat box while your husband's at work, and you're instantly connected with anyone you choose. And of course the men we meet on the Net are seemingly perfect. Aren't we all?

We all put our best images forward, but behind doors we live in the real world where Photoshop doesn't exist, Google isn't our voices, and a backspace button can't undo a bad day. Fantasy is hard to compete with. What does it tell us when we see other husbands doing the things that our husbands don't do?

What it should tell us is that God is blessing our marriages in a unique way. By following His lead and keeping our eyes focused on the path before us, we find contentment and peace.

Consider horses. Have you ever been to the races? I've only been once, but I've also watched the movie *Seabiscuit*, if that counts. I used to wonder what the shades on their eyes were all about until Michael explained their significance. One of the biggest distractions in a race can be the crowd; another is the other contestants. Many trainers believe that blinders (also known as winkers) are beneficial to racehorses because they encourage the animals to pay attention to the race ahead. In much the same way, we are far more productive when we focus on the plan ahead rather than check out the competition and the crowds that they draw.

Comparing our husbands or our marriages to those of others is pointless because we're all walking different paths. We haven't come from the same places, we're not dealing with the same circumstances, and—here's my seamstress voice talking again—we're not cut from the same cloth. Let's face it.

Some of us are fuzzy dice material, and some of us are suede, but every one of us has a story of her or his own that unfolds with each passing day.

God gifts men in numerous ways: intelligence, strength, talent, skill, wisdom, courage, sensitivity, humor, financial success, and the list goes on. Men might have one or several of these gifts, but I have yet to meet a man who possesses all of them.

God didn't create perfect human beings. You, me, our husbands—we're all sinners saved by grace. Every one of us comes complete with flaws that we struggle to overcome. Even the apostle Paul struggled with the flesh, and he wrote about his struggles so we'd understand our need for grace.

You have expectations of a man on the one hand and your husband on the other, who you've come to realize isn't all that you expected. You wanted fun on Friday nights, not sluggish on Saturdays. You wanted courageous, not weak. And you wanted a man who'd walk through the door with a dozen roses after work, but instead you get a dozen reasons why he's too tired to take you out.

The problem here isn't your husband; it's that your level of expectation for him is outshining his character. When you measure him against the weight of expectation, you are left with an unbalanced scale.

Accepting a person for who he or she is doesn't mean that you excuse sin. I'd never ask or want you to do that. What I am asking you to do is to look past the human frailty of a man to seek his beauty by removing the weight of expectation you hold. I'm asking that you walk in the grace of messy, beautiful love.

THE CHALLENGE

Pay attention to the good qualities in your husband. What makes him different? What do you love about him? Take note of the good things he does and the kind things he says. Carefully notice the ways that he expresses his love, even if they seem insignificant at the time.

Start building him up by reminding him how much you appreciate him and the many little things that you love about him.

| SIX |

Step Back and Allow Him to Lead

LAST NIGHT, MY DAUGHTER, MADISON, made tacos for dinner. After the meal she spent the evening in the kitchen cutting up veggies and frying beef for a pot of stew. Not bad for a fifteen-year-old, huh? She worked in the kitchen from the time she got home from school until it was time for bed. Well, sort of. I let her work at the dining room table so she could watch television while peeling potatoes, cutting carrots, and slicing celery.

You know what she said to me around 10:00 p.m.? "Thanks for letting me make the stew, Mom."

Thank me? Uh, thank *you* for spending your evening serving your family! How in the world did I ever get such an incredible daughter? My only answer is that this is a *God* thing.

The thing about God is that while He gives us incredible gifts, He also gives us the opportunity to nurture those gifts, otherwise known as being a good steward of what we have.

I've never loved cooking. You wouldn't know it if you saw my apron collection, though. Four of them are hanging in the kitchen right now, my favorite being the Grace & Gratitude apron. It's one of the prettiest things my kitchen has ever seen next to the vintage pay phone. The skirt is ruffled with layers of colorful fabric, complete with the words, *A grateful soul is truly blessed.* Madison and I get along well for the most part, but we love to fight over who gets that apron. She usually wins.

I can cook well, but I've never enjoyed it in the same way that she does. Here is the way I see it: I work in the kitchen for an hour or two on something that is gobbled up in five minutes. Where is the fun in that?

Madison sees it a different way. To her it's worth spending an entire night in the kitchen if she knows that someone in the family will enjoy what she makes. By the way, beef stew is my favorite. It used to be stroganoff, but lately beef stew is taking the lead.

The question is, how did she get to this point? And why didn't I ever get there? Aside from the fact that we're two different people, we were nurtured in two different ways.

My mom grew up in a family of eighteen children. Of those eighteen, my mom was one of two who baked bread every day. If she had something to do or someplace to go, it was her responsibility to make sure that the bread was made *before* she went out. Some days she'd trade up. She'd take on two shifts in a row so she could have a day off. In addition to baking, she cooked for the family day in and day out. Their recipes were standard family favorites, and there was no time to experiment with new things. If you like soup, you'd love my mom! She can make soup out of anything. Give her a bag of rocks, and she'll have a pot of soup for you by the end of the day along with a loaf of fresh bread. Vegetable soup, chicken noodle soup, butter soup, mushroom soup, onion soup, summa borscht, beet borscht, bean soup—you name it, she makes it. And she makes it *well*.

As a result of this upbringing, she was armed with some of the best recipes. Unfortunately, they weren't written in a book, and they didn't include "a cup of this and a tablespoon of that." They were "a handful of this and some of that." When it came to cooking, Mom didn't have to measure or read; she just *knew*. And while she mixed a bit of this and some of that, she worked quickly to get the job done.

She always wore aprons, which is probably why I still love them so much. They had a way of dressing up any outfit. Not that she needed any dressing up since she was, and still is, the kind of woman who keeps herself pretty. Slender and tall with chestnut-colored hair and chocolate brown eyes, she has classic beauty. Think Judy Garland in the *Wizard of Oz*. Not overly done, just done up enough to keep turning Dad's head. Why he didn't have neck problems I'll never know.

She was a June Cleaver type who did it all, and did it all *well*. There was never a pile of laundry to be found. She and Dad had six girls, and each of us had a dresser full of clean clothes always folded and fresh. Every pair of socks had a match, and every pair of underwear was folded just right. Her whites were white, her blacks were black, and her colors were vibrant.

It was her mission to make our home pretty. Whether she was sliding the couch from one wall to the other or refilling a vase with fresh flowers, she was always changing things up. The only thing she never seemed to change was the way that she cooked. She did things a particular way because they just didn't taste quite right to her if they were done differently.

Being the creative type that I am, my idea of cooking was much different from hers. My desire has always been to create new recipes and to experiment a little by changing things up. But the kitchen wasn't my canvas. It wasn't a place where I could create. Cooking was a chore that was done the same way day in and day out. Get in the kitchen and help Mom by washing the dishes and setting the table, so she can get the job done.

My sister Bonnie started baking in her teens. She learned to make carrot and spice cake at school, so Mom encouraged her to bake on the weekends. The rule was that if Bonnie was willing to bake, I had to clean up the mess. Lucky for me. Unfortunately, her love for baking increased while my love for the kitchen decreased. I couldn't stand the smell of cake and cookies and didn't eat them for years. However, I could really wash mixing bowls!

I was determined to change things with my kids. The kitchen is our space to have fun and create. This is the place where memories are made and new recipes are discovered. This is the space where we bond as a family. We're not perfect when it comes to the food that we make, but we enjoy the process of cooking together and enjoying a meal. Did I mention that I make the best spaghetti sauce ever? I do.

A few years ago I went out of town for a couple of days to attend a writing conference. I think that Madison must have been about eleven, and while I was gone, she was helping Michael cook for the boys. If having three brothers has taught her anything, it's that men appreciate good food. When I got home from the conference, Michael told me that Madison wanted to start cooking the dinner meals. She was ready and willing to take on the job. My first thought was that he was out of his mind. There was no way this idea would stick for more than a day. My second thought was how inexperienced she was. Would we be eating cereal day after day? Was toast on the menu? Not taking them too seriously, I decided to step back and give her free rein for a while. She wasn't perfect at first—nobody is—but four years later I have a young chef on my hands.

She doesn't do all the cooking by any means, but she enjoys it enough to experiment with recipes a few times a week.

In so many ways, taking a step back in my kitchen reminds me of the way I've taken a step back in our marriage. I've given up my right to be in charge so that Michael can lead us in the best way he knows how. I'd like to say that I've given up my *desire* to lead, but I think that deep inside there's always going to be the human desire to take over and say, "Look, you're doing this wrong!" After all, we're two different people with two different ideas of how things should be done. What if he fails? What if he makes the wrong choice? The truth is that he *will*. Any of us would, and we do. The bottom line is that we're all a work in progress, growing and learning every step of the way.

If I want my husband to grow into a strong man who is ready and willing to lead our family, I need to allow him that room to grow. I need to allow him to make grilled cheese until he works his way up to beef stew. I haven't always been willing to do this. As you probably guessed from the first chapter, I've been a rebellious brat. But grace has a way of turning my eyes to the Lord where I see a plan that's much better than mine. One in which a wife steps down in humility and allows her husband to lead.

My purpose is to glorify God in the way that I live by walking in obedience to His Word.

That Word tells me, "As the church is subject unto

Christ, so let the wives be to their own husbands in every thing. Husbands, love your wives, even as Christ also loved the church, and gave himself for it" (Eph. 5:24–25).

When we consider everything that Jesus did for us, we can see the responsibility that is asked of our husbands. They whipped Him, they spat in His face, they ridiculed Him, and they nailed Him to a cross. His response to all that was *grace*. He didn't come to condemn us; instead He lowered Himself to the level of a servant and washed His disciples' feet. He came in humility that we might be saved.

Yes, the Bible tells us that the husband is the head of the wife and that the wife should submit to his authority. With that in mind we should remember that submission is a choice that we make. It's not something that is or should be imposed on us by another person. It's our response to God's love. It is a choice we make out of obedience to God because ultimately everything we do should focus on Him and His will. There's a reason we do it, and that reason is to please God.

We see the beauty of submission since the beginning of time when Sarah obeyed Abraham, calling him lord (1 Peter 3:6).

Sarah brought glory to God through obedience to her faith. She wasn't perfect; in fact she laughed when she heard that God was going to bless her with a child. At her age? She was old, and as far as she was concerned, it was impossible.

God doesn't use perfect people to build His kingdom; He uses those who walk in obedience to Him, but in order to do that we must submit to His will for our lives. Samuel said, "Hath the LORD as great delight in burnt offerings and sacrifices, as in obeying the voice of the LORD? Behold, to obey is better than sacrifice, and to hearken than the fat of rams" (1 Sam. 15:22). You see, it's easy to make a sacrifice to the Lord—go to church on Sunday, put money in the collection plate, send a box of toys to Goodwill, and the list goes on—but to bring our lives under *obedience* to God is where the real challenge lies.

We live in a society where hundreds of thousands of people say that they believe in Jesus, but how many of us are willing to walk in obedience to His commands?

What if the wisdom of God doesn't make sense to your situation? What if it doesn't feel good to submit to the Lord? What if it doesn't feel good to submit to your husband?

Some follow the wisdom of God, but others start looking around for an easier way. Scripture is bent out of shape to justify a *better* way of doing things.

Those who treasure Jesus Christ honor His authority in their lives and walk in obedience to the faith.

This mind-set of submission is completely foolish to our society, which isn't surprising at all.

Paul wrote: "We preach Christ crucified, unto the Jews a stumblingblock, and unto the Greeks foolishness; but unto them which are called, both Jews and Greeks, Christ the power of God, and the wisdom of God. Because the foolishness of God is wiser than men; and the weakness of God is stronger than men" (1 Cor. 1:23–25). It may seem foolish to many when I submit to my husband, but the foolishness of God is wiser than ours.

Are we wives second class? Absolutely not, and no, every argument isn't our fault. But there will be times when we communicate in every way possible, and our husbands still won't see things the way that we do. That's when we can honor God by stepping back in humility and letting our husbands take the lead.

Readers often ask me what they should do when their husbands aren't equipped to lead. It's a good question, but in answering it, we have to realize that regardless of how mature he is or how experienced he is, he's a work in progress. Isn't every husband?

Could there possibly be any man who is fully equipped to lead a family? Or is it possible that God is ready and willing to equip those He calls?

The minute you stand in the middle, refusing to believe that God's plan for man is better than yours, you take away the opportunity for God to bless your husband in this area.

I want to be Michael's helper, but I also want to be an encourager by allowing him to lead our family. I need to trust God in this area of my life, even when my pride tells me I shouldn't.

If you look at your husband and say, "Whoa, this man can't balance a checkbook! How could he possibly handle our finances?" offer to help by working out a budget with him. Letting him lead your family doesn't mean that you aren't or shouldn't be part of the planning process. By all means you should. God created Eve because He saw that Adam was alone and that he needed a helper. You are an essential part of your marriage.

Submission is a vital part of the marriage covenant that cannot be overlooked or discarded. It's a step that we take in obedience to God for the purpose of bringing glory to God in our marriages. Although submission is the beautiful, perfect will of God, it should never be misused. In other words, we should never be abused.

I don't approach this topic with naivety or insensitivity. I've seen the best, and I've seen the worst. I was once married to a man who abused me. Thankfully, that was a lifetime ago, *before* I met Michael and *before* I understood the beauty of submission and what it entailed. Nobody has the right to hurt you or to force you to sin against God. So if you are in danger, please speak to someone about it. Get help before you get hurt.

The kind of submission that I'm talking about brings glory to God. Whether our husbands are searching or saved, we can honor our Lord by living in such a way that draws them closer to Him.

> But let it be the hidden man of the heart, in that which
> is not corruptible, even the ornament of a meek and quiet

spirit, which is in the sight of God of great price. For after this manner in the old time the holy women also, who trusted in God, adorned themselves, being in subjection unto their own husbands. (1 Peter 3:4–5)

So what about those husbands who don't want to lead a family? After all, we're cut from different cloth, right? It stands to reason that some will be leaders and others would prefer to sit back and let you make decisions. Here's the thing: if he tells you that he wants you to make the decisions, then he's made a decision right there.

I smile when I get letters from readers who say, "My husband told me that he doesn't want me to submit to him, so I can't." My answer is, "Well, you better obey his wishes then."

It's kind of cute to see couples trying to figure this out, but it's an incredible blessing when you see couples who are willing to step down in humility and yield to the will of the Lord. I think, *I wish I had your understanding of Scripture when I was that young.* My pilgrimage would have taken a different path, and my marriage would have been blessed by the fruit of obedience.

You see, I knew in my head that I was called to submit to my husband, but I hadn't taken it to heart because doing so would have meant that I had to lay down my life as I knew it for the good of my marriage. It was easy to be submissive in some areas of my life—and I did so joyfully—but I wasn't ready to let go completely. When I finally realized that my marriage was crumbling beneath the weight of my sin, I understood that it was not only worth fighting for; it was worth dying for. If I was going to make this marriage work, I'd have to give up my silly notions that I know what's best for my life and trust God with my future. Free-falling into the arms of my Savior, I chose His will over mine.

I've come to the understanding that submission runs deeper than merely stepping back so my husband can lead. It's an act of yielding my life in submission to the Father who rewards those who seek Him. Regardless of who is balancing the checkbook or deciding on the color of drapes, we must remember that marriage is a testimony of God's relationship to the world. When we honor our spouses, we bring glory to God.

There's a saying that goes like this: "The world doesn't read the Bible; it reads Christians." What are your actions saying? What does your marriage say about your relationship with the Lord? Is it something to be desired?

It might seem silly to think that your response to marriage could lead anyone to the saving knowledge of Christ. But the truth is that we don't do the saving; *God* does. All that He asks is that we walk in obedience to Him. In doing so we are lights on a hill.

We live in a messed-up world where values have been tossed to the side. So many people barely know what Christianity is anymore. God has become whatever we *want* Him to be as long as He serves our purpose and fulfills our lust for more of this world. Somewhere in the middle of all this mess, a searching heart finds a marriage that is blessed with beautiful love. A marriage that doesn't conform to this world but is transformed by the wisdom of God so that it proves what is acceptable and perfect in His sight. Somewhere in the middle of all this mess, that person finds hope.

The wisdom of God is foolish to men, but who among men can hang the sun and the moon in the sky? Who among men can breathe life into man? We can't even *begin* to understand the depth of the wisdom of God.

THE CHALLENGE

Pray for your husband, asking that God will equip him to lead your family. If you haven't done so already, examine yourself to see whether there are areas of your marriage where you should step back so that he can step forward. Keep the lines of communication open for healthy discussion, but on those days when you can't come to a united decision? Humbly step back, and allow his choices to stand.

SEVEN

Handle Your Conflict Wisely

IT WAS 7:00 A.M., THE KIDS WERE DRAGGING THEM-selves out of bed, and Michael was in the kitchen searching for a spoon to go with his bowl of cereal. That man loves his breakfast, let me tell you!

Our cupboards are filled with oversized bowls because an average-sized bowl doesn't cut it for him. Neither does an average-sized box of cereal. Michael goes for the biggest box he can find, and even *that* isn't big enough.

From the sound of the clanking, the drawers slamming open and shut, and the occasional huff, I could tell that Michael's search for a spoon wasn't all that successful.

"Who ran the dishwasher last night?" he hollered from the kitchen. "I think it's time we sat the family down for a meeting!"

It wasn't so much his words as it was the tone of his voice that told me this wasn't going to be the happiest morning for any of us. He was furious and not about to let this one slide. Out of fairness to Michael, I have to say that I agreed with his evaluation of the dishes. One of the kids had put a pan of scalloped potatoes into the dishwasher without bothering to scrape it first. When I pulled the "clean" pan out, it still had a layer or two of potatoes on it, only now they were washed, rinsed, and dried onto the pan. Worst mess I've ever had, which is pretty bad considering that I've seen a few doozies before. That morning every cup, fork, and spoon had a layer of grime on it. Everything needed to soak, which makes for twice the work that it was in the first place. Ugh!

I agreed that the dishes were in a sad state, but I wasn't so agreeable with Michael's attitude in general. Like anyone else, he can be a glass half-full kind of guy once in a while, but that morning he was a glass half-full of poison. Within minutes everyone was setting him off.

Graham couldn't do chores properly, Nathaniel was in bed sick because "he's been eating too much junk food," and Madison was taking too long to get out of bed because "she stays up too late!" They were all important things to consider—and certainly talk about—but in a span of five minutes? It was early, and I was barely awake. He plunked down on the couch with breakfast in hand and started in with one problem after another, barely taking a moment to breathe between thoughts, never mind digging into his cereal.

Wanting desperately to change the subject and get off on a better foot, I let seven little words slip out of my mouth and into the air: "Are you going to finish your breakfast?"

Grabbing his bowl, he rose from the sofa, stamped his way up the stairs, and hollered back, "You might as well just tell me to shut up! It's the same thing."

With that the house was silent. Even the Rice Krispies knew better than to snap, crackle, or pop. He was fueled by anger, and all I had said were those seven little words. Gently, I might add.

Here's the thing. Michael tends to skip a meal when he's upset, which doesn't help when someone's feeling a bit cranky. His cereal was getting soggy, he had a long day ahead, and I sensed that eating was the best thing he could do. I knew that anything I said would set him off that morning. I could see that the anger in his face was hungry for a fight, and I was his likely opponent.

I tucked Nathaniel back in, got Madison and Graham ready for school, and went upstairs to our room. Walking into the bedroom, I noticed the soggy, untouched bowl of cereal was resting on his nightstand. Michael was in the shower getting ready for work, and I crawled back into bed for a nap.

Maybe I was tired, or maybe I just wanted to wake up and start the day over—either one sounded inviting to me.

Resting my head on the pillow, I got to thinking about how angry I was. Who was he to treat me that way? The old me would have marched into the bathroom and confronted him right then and there. Wait, back that up. He wouldn't have gotten up those stairs without a good fight. I would have made sure of that!

I was angry at the way I was treated, and I had every right to be. Who wants to wake up to someone snapping at her? Who wants to face the day with a long list of complaints? Who wants to live in a house where she isn't respected?

Years ago I would have reacted to his anger by lashing out at him, and we would have hammered things out right then and there. But the new me—the one who chooses to walk by the Spirit and live by the wisdom of God—took a different path that is paved with forgiveness and grace, a path that calls us to be tenderhearted and forgiving to one another for the sake of our Lord Jesus Christ.

Let me interject here that I don't walk this path perfectly by any means. I'm a work in progress that's stumbling through this life and making my way through it by *grace*. I definitely know how to make a mess of my life, and I've seen what choosing to live by my wisdom has done. This time I'm following His. Choosing God's will for my marriage calls me to put down the weapons of warfare and pick up the instrument of peace, which is that of a kind and gentle heart.

It's never easy to walk in humility or to exercise patience, but as it is with any exercise, the more we flex those muscles, the stronger we get. We have to dig into God, and if we're feeling let down and discouraged, we have to dig deeper yet. In order to grow patient we must practice *being* patient time and again; but doing so is always difficult in the moment, isn't it? Each time I fail, I'm reminded of how human I am and just how big the grace of God is.

Laying my head on the pillow, I closed my eyes, trying my best to relax. My heart was heavy and my spirit crushed. The pug had just found a spot next to my tummy when the bathroom door opened and Michael emerged. With eyes closed, I heard his footsteps move across the room and over to my side of the bed. Then sitting down beside me, he reached out for my hand.

Part of me wanted to hang on to my anger. A big part of me. I wanted to ignore him and pretend I was sleeping. I wanted him to hurt as much as I did and to feel the sting of my pain. But a small voice inside instructed me otherwise.

Sometimes that voice—the one led by wisdom—is quiet. It struggles to be heard over the cries of the flesh that wrestle against the Spirit within us. But if we truly want peace in marriage, we must walk by the Spirit in obedience to our Lord. Turning toward him, I opened my eyes and responded by squeezing his hand.

"I'm so sorry," he said. "You didn't deserve any of that."

Looking into his deep blue eyes, I could tell that he meant every word. He really was sorry that his anger had gotten the best of him. He was sorry that he had taken it out on me the way he had. And I loved him for telling me so.

That afternoon he called me from work to apologize yet again. "I love you," he said, "and I'm so sorry about this morning."

That evening he came down with the flu, and with that I realized why he had been so irritable in the morning. It wasn't like him to be that angry or frustrated, but I imagine his body was wearing him down.

We don't always know what's going on in the heart of a person, and we can't even begin to guess why he or she does the things that he or she does. But we do control what's going on in our hearts and what *we* choose to do.

Ask the rest of the world how they handle their anger, and you'll hear something like, "If he doesn't like it, show him the door!" When marriages are broken, many people just toss them aside. Gone are the days when people stuck together because they believed that a marriage covenant was more than a piece of paper. Gone are the days when men and women stood by the promise they made "till death do us part." And gone are the days when people knelt at the side of their beds, bringing their marriage before God in prayer.

I thank God every day for a husband who doesn't live by the standard of this world. His testimony of humility and grace has drawn me closer to Christ than anything else has.

Just imagine the effect of your testimony on the world when you're walking in obedience to Christ. Marriage is a symphony of grace orchestrated by an almighty God, reflecting His love to mankind. One can't help being drawn to its beauty.

But we have a choice. We can live by the standard of this world, which is characterized by selfish ambition and pride, or we can choose God's standard for marriage, which is perfect in every way. Sure it will still be messy at times because we're growing and learning, but when we yield our hearts to God's will, we experience His incomparable blessing on our marriages. That's a beautiful thing.

Every day we're given a choice to either walk by the wisdom of God or yield to our sinful desire. Do we have a right to be angry? Absolutely, but we must handle our anger in a way that is pleasing to God and conforms to His will.

Here's a letter I received from a reader who was frustrated with change, but more importantly with the disappointment that came with it. I offered her encouragement by reminding her that while we're called to exercise love, we also have a Savior who we should call on.

Dear Darlene,

I believe in submitting to my husband because the Bible tells me to. I do understand that and I embrace it. I have a confession, however, and maybe it's just me? I don't always feel like submitting to him. In fact some days I'm only doing it because I feel that it's my Christian duty as a wife. I feel terrible because I know that I should enjoy submitting to him, but I feel like my flesh is at war with my spirit.

And there's more. My husband and I recently had a disagreement. After talking things out with him we came to a unified decision, which was good. The problem is that he changed his mind without telling me and chose to handle things his way.

I don't really need to go into the details of what happened because it's all said and done now. The problem is that I'm angry at the way things turned out. Do I have a "right" to be angry? Or should I stifle those feelings for the good of my marriage?

I've prayed about it, but I can't shake this feeling of hurt and frustration. I'd like to talk to my husband about it, but I'm not sure if that's the right thing to do or if I need to let go and move on.

I hope you can help.

Frustrated

Dear Frustrated,

Thank you so much for your letter and for sharing your heart with me. You talked about whether or not you had a "right" to be angry. Here's the thing. God knows that we'll definitely get angry from time to time. The Bible says to be angry and sin not. Here's a great passage of Scripture in its entirety:

> You heard about Christ and were taught in him in accordance with the truth that is in Jesus. You were taught, with regard to your former way of life, to put off your old self, which is being corrupted by its deceitful desires; to be made new in the attitude of your minds; and to put on the new self, created to be like God in true righteousness and holiness. Therefore each of you must put off falsehood and speak truthfully to your neighbor, for we are all members of one body. "In your anger do not sin": Do not let the sun go down while you are still angry, and do not give the devil a foothold. (Eph. 4:21–27 NIV)

When I look at that passage, I see that while God understands that we will get angry, we are to guard our thoughts in the process so that the devil doesn't get a foothold. Satan loves to get his foot into the door of our marriages any time we leave it open a crack!

You said, "I don't always feel like submitting to him. In fact some days I'm only doing it because I feel that it's my Christian duty as a wife."

I can't help being reminded of our Savior's walk to the cross. Remember in the garden just hours before His death He prayed, asking that this cup (the suffering) be removed from Him: "Father, if thou be willing, remove this cup from me: nevertheless not my will, but thine, be done" (Luke 22:42).

And so we see that He lived to please God. He wasn't living to please Himself or mankind. He was submitting to the plan of salvation because of His obedience to the Father. We submit to our husbands to reflect the covenant between Christ and His church.

I think that the core of your question was, should I talk to my husband about this or let go and move on? I see a few things in here that can guide us through these frustrating times (and remember that we all get frustrated). We must be careful to guard our hearts and our minds from the temptation to sin in our anger.

Notice the part that says, "speak truthfully to your

neighbor." Communication is so important in a marriage, and the best way to keep the lines of communication open is to approach our husbands with humility and grace.

Was he wrong? He might very well have been. I don't know the entire situation, and even if I did, I wouldn't have the wisdom to judge his actions. But I do know that we can't accept another person's imperfections until we have mastered the lesson of understanding our own. Until we see what God's grace and forgiveness have done for us.

A good rule of thumb for keeping our thoughts in line is to line ourselves up with Paul's lesson on love: "Love is patient, love is kind. It does not envy, it does not boast, it is not proud. It does not dishonor others, it is not self-seeking, it is not easily angered, it keeps no record of wrongs. Love does not delight in evil but rejoices with the truth. It always protects, always trusts, always hopes, always perseveres" (1 Cor. 13:4–7 NIV).

And let's not forget the power of prayer or use it as a last resort. We don't have the ability to change another person; people have enough trouble trying to change themselves. The truth is that God is able to do abundantly more than we ask or think.

We don't always have to understand how or why things happen the way that they do. Our job is to leave our burden in His capable hands and do our best to walk in truth.

Blessings,

Darlene

Communication is a vital part of growing together (and we'll talk more about that in the next chapter), but it's important that while we share our concerns, we do so with wisdom and love.

When Michael was angry, I knew that communicating right then and there would only add fuel to the fire. He was too angry to hear me, and I was coming from a place of anger too. I might have said things I would regret later, and if I didn't, I'm sure that he would have.

If he hadn't come to my side of the bed and apologized, I would have phoned him at work later that morning to see how he was and to extend a hand of grace. I've found that offering grace is the first and most important step in opening a door to communication.

When we walk in humility, treating others with more love and respect than we might think they deserve, we aren't choosing the way of weakness; we're choosing the way of strength under control.

You see, it's easy to fly off the handle and let our emotions get the best of us. But wise is the woman who gets the best of her emotions. Walking in wisdom and strength, she keeps them under control.

I can't promise you that this will be easy, but I can say that marriage—the way that God intended it to be—is a treasure worth fighting for.

THE CHALLENGE

Learn to follow the voice of wisdom and tune out the cries of the flesh. The next time that you are feeling angry, pouty, or frustrated, resolve to handle your emotions in a way that is pleasing to God. Be willing to walk in humility when it's required of you, and make choices that will unite you and your husband as a couple and draw you closer to God.

| EIGHT |

Communicate with Loving Respect

IF YOU REMEMBER EIGHTH GRADE BIOLOGY class, you might remember the following lesson: when you touch a hot element, your hand sends a message to the brain. The brain decides the best plan of action and immediately sends a message back to your hand, telling you to move it quickly. Without the nervous system, you'd be burned, bruised, and blind. It's one of the most vital functions of the body.

In the same way, communication is vital to every relationship. It's the system that sends a message from one to the other, much like the hand to the head. If we don't communicate our desires to each other, we can't expect them to be fulfilled.

It should be easy enough, but the problem is that men and women tend to communicate differently. It makes sense since we are two very different kinds of people. Physically it's obvious. A man's body, voice, and strength are undeniably different from a woman's. Less noticeable are the differences in the way of thinking. For example, a man desires to provide for his family and has a need for respect. A woman tends to enjoy nesting (did someone mention Pinterest?) and knowing that she is loved. Of course no two men are exactly alike, and no two women are exactly alike. Generally speaking, however, there is a broad range of similarities within the sexes.

When we go over to another couple's house for dinner, depending on whether it's our first time there, they may invite us on a tour of their home. Let the record show that I'd never ask for a tour, but if I'm invited on one I'm all over that like peanut butter on a bib. I absolutely love checking out trinkets, looking at photos, and gleaning a few decorating ideas.

My friend Stephanie is good for that. Her house is filled with thrift-store finds, upcycled gadgets, and homemade crafts. Every corner has a little something to see. Last Christmas we were invited over to a friend's house for dinner along with a few other couples from church. If you are the crafty or decorating type, you would love her place! I enjoyed every inch of her wall space from the moment I walked through the door.

After dinner they invited us on a little tour, and I got to further check out the decor. One of my favorite things she does is recycle old books. The little trees she made from them got me wondering why I threw out a box of vintage books last year. I knew I should have held onto them!

By the time we women got to the basement, we ran into our husbands who were chatting by the furnace room door. While we were poking around in her craft collection, they were discussing wiring, plumbing, and a solid foundation. I don't think they ever got up to the bedroom to see the handmade garland that decorated the walls. So pretty!

While the women were absorbed in the small touches that made their house a home, the guys wanted to know what made that home a house, and so they lingered in the basement, banging on pipes, checking out beams, and following wires.

It's always been that way. Anytime we've purchased a house, I've spent the majority of the time thinking about what colors I'd paint the rooms and where we'd put our furniture. On the other hand, Michael always wants to get into the basement to examine the structure. He commits the building specs to memory and later discusses them with the guys over coffee. Meanwhile I call my sisters to tell them how many bedrooms it has, what the cupboards are like, and what color the walls are.

"How many square feet is it?"

"Hold on, I'll ask Michael," I say.

Three weeks ago my daughter and I went to IKEA with

my oldest son. It was a dream come true for Madison and me, who had to touch every blanket and walk through every door in the place. Meanwhile Brendan was saying, "Oh, man. This is painful. Get me out of here now!" Lucky for us it's set up in such a way that shoppers have to walk through the entire store before leaving. Not so lucky for him.

The fact that we're different is a good thing, really. I need someone who's concerned about the structure of our house. After all, these things need to be considered before even purchasing a house. But Michael also needs someone who's passionate about making our house a comfy little home; someone who gets excited about the color of drapes and whether the pillows will match. I bring beauty into his life, and he brings structure into mine.

Yes, being different is good, but it's not always easy. Learning to communicate with your husband is a lifelong process of learning who he is and what makes him tick.

During the early years of marriage, if we had an argument, Michael usually asked, "Are you mad at me?"

While we were in the midst of a fight, I wasn't angry at him. The truth is that my feelings were hurt. So my answer to that question was usually no. I didn't want to tell him that I was hurt because I wanted him to love me enough to figure it out. Silly, I know! If he dropped it right there and didn't try to find out what was bothering me, I'd start getting angry at him. Then I'd be both angry and hurt. See how complicated I can be?

If I can't figure myself out, how in the world is my husband supposed to? Women are complicated. I know because I am one. Men, on the other hand, aren't so complicated, but since men and women don't think the same way, it takes awhile to figure them out.

Being with someone over the years has its benefits. Over time you learn how to read someone's actions better than you could read his words. According to some studies, nonverbal communication represents more than 65 percent of communication, with many sources citing statistics as high as 90 percent.[1] Whatever the percentage, we know that our primary source of communication is through body language.

When Michael is bothered about something, I can usually see it right away by looking at his eyes. He's unfocused, and he looks to his left. If he's really frustrated, he goes on a mad cleaning spree. He'll walk into the kitchen and start loading the dishwasher. I can hear the dishes clanging and the cupboard doors closing.

The way I used to handle it is that I'd rush in there and say, "Stop cleaning. I want to talk to you." The way I handle it now is that I let him clean for a little while first, and then I go in. That way we both win. He blows off a little steam, and I get a clean kitchen.

I don't know what my "tells" are exactly, but I do know that he can read them loud and clear. If I'm really upset, I'll go lie in the bed. He always comes up, sits on the side of the bed, and talks to me until things are talked out. I don't know what I'd do if he wasn't persistent enough to follow me upstairs and sit there waiting for me. I love that about him!

In many ways things have gotten so much easier because I've come to learn who he is and how to read his emotions. But like everyone else, we still have our bouts of miscommunication. I can't tell you how many times that we got our wires crossed while out shopping and ended up in a fight. Okay, I can. Maybe five? But it felt like a hundred. We'd go to the mall, plan to meet at a certain place at a certain time, and somehow one of us would get the location mixed up. How did that keep happening? We'd both stand there waiting for more than an hour. Of course this was before cell phones.

All I could think of was how insensitive he was for not showing up. How could someone do that? Was his time more precious than mine? How much was a cab? Maybe I should call one and take off? Maybe I should teach him a lesson? And while I looked at my watch, I'd think of a thousand and one things I'd say to him once we got home.

Finally, we'd spot each other wandering through the mall. After exchanging a few words of frustration, I could see that he had a valid excuse for not showing up. But you know what? When you're that angry, it's hard to let it go. Something inside you *wants* to hang on to your anger, as if holding on to it will redeem your frustration. It doesn't. It just prolongs that ugly feeling of anger.

Even with cell phones, communication can be a problem. My daughter started high school this year, so we got her a cell phone to call us when she needed a ride home or had to stay late after school. The second week of school, I went to pick her up at the bus stop at 4:10. She wasn't there. I figured that maybe her bus was late, so I tried again about ten minutes later. Seeing that she still wasn't there, I put dinner on and got busy in the kitchen. Three more times I put dinner aside, hopped in the car, and went to see if she was at the bus stop or walking home. Nothing.

Around 6:00 I told Michael that Madison was due home at 4:00, and I hadn't heard from her yet. I left about ten messages on her cell phone, but she wasn't picking up. When 6:30 rolled around and still I heard nothing, I started to worry.

That's when I said to myself, *If she isn't hurt, she's in a boatload of trouble! That girl has some answering to do.* And yeah, I was angry.

Michael popped in at the other high school where her friends were playing basketball. We figured that maybe she went there and didn't bother to call. Sure enough, she was there with her cell phone and its ringer turned off.

When she got in the door, I started to lecture her on the importance of communication. My first question was, "Why didn't you call?"

She replied, "I did call, but you didn't answer, so I left a message."

I had been out of the house for about ten minutes at that time picking up the boys from their school when I missed the call on the home phone. Instead of trying to catch me on my cell or trying the home phone again, she gave up. I hadn't even thought about checking the messages since I had my cell phone on me the entire time.

And so I was angry, but yeah, she had a valid excuse. Although her intentions were good, our communication was lost. Again and again I stressed the importance to her of communication and how both of us have to be on the same page. It's been a few months now since she's started high school and been using a cell phone, so we've had a few months to even out the bumps.

Looking at her, I'm reminded of communication between young couples and what a learning curve it can be. As good as intentions might be, they often get overshadowed by perceptions or misunderstandings. We need to keep listening and watching so that we can learn the language of our spouses.

If the hand doesn't say to the brain, "This is hot," the brain will go about other business while the hand is destroyed by the heat. In order for two to function as one, they need to be in communication with each other.

The fact is, we will get angry, but the key to a good relationship is being able to relay that frustration in love. A good rule of thumb? Love your husband enough to trust his intentions. Rather than get upset at something he's done, give him the benefit of the doubt and ask yourself if it's a malicious act on his part or if it's a matter of miscommunication. Getting along has everything to do with putting aside your desire to have things your way so that you might strengthen the bond of unity.

What happens when we don't communicate? When we don't tell our husbands what we expect, what we need, and how much we hurt? Like any wound that is left untreated, it risks getting infected.

Take my pug Bailey for instance. My puppies are like all little pugs. They have a billion folds in their faces and ears. Pugs are known for their wrinkles, but they're also known to get infections because of the dirt that collects within them. As cute and cuddly as they are, I have to ensure that I clean their faces and ears well.

Since Bailey (my older pug) is a 24/7 lapdog, this really isn't difficult to maintain. While she's lying on my lap, I'll flip her ears over and check them several times a day. I do it without even thinking about it anymore, and I don't think she notices either.

A few months ago I noticed a little problem—she was scratching feverishly at her left ear. Before even flipping it open I could smell the infection. How did I miss that? Looking back on it later, I realized that she always lies on her left side when she cuddles up on the couch. Therefore I'm always cleaning her right ear, ignoring the left. The poor little thing!

We picked up some medicine for her, and within a few days she was back to her old self. I wasn't impressed with myself for overlooking such an important part of her health, but I did learn a little something about infections: (1) left untreated, they spread fast, and (2) prevention is better than medicine.

Apply that wisdom to your marriage, and you will see why communication is important. If you leave infections untreated, they can quickly spread and get out of control. But by keeping the lines of communication open, you prevent feelings of anger and frustration from building up to be more than they should be.

Here's a letter that I received from a reader who was struggling to understand the difference between nagging and communicating. The root of her question was, do we have a right to speak up when we're not happy with a situation?

Dear Darlene,

I'm having a little trouble understanding the difference between nagging and my right to speak up when I should.

We've been married for fifteen years. During the first few years of marriage, my husband seemed to enjoy taking care of our house. He would fix little things that were broken and didn't mind pitching in. Unfortunately things have changed. He's always busy at work, and the house is a far second, which usually means that things don't get done.

I wouldn't complain except that things are falling apart, and I'm frustrated. It's like he either doesn't notice or doesn't care anymore. I've tried sliding it into conversation, but even that's not what it used to be.

So here's my question. Do I have a right to speak up? Do I have a voice in this marriage, or am I supposed to be quiet and let him live the way he wants to live?

Thanks so much,

Holding My Tongue

Dear Holding My Tongue,

Thank you for your letter. I'm so blessed that you are seeking God's way for your marriage. Communication is important to both men and women. We don't always see it that way because men communicate differently. Many women say that their husbands won't talk to them, but if you stop to watch the way he expresses himself, after a while you'll become more familiar with his method of communication.

It could be any one of several reasons why your husband doesn't tend to duties around the house. I could guess and guess again, but without knowing him and your particular situation I would probably be off the mark.

So the best thing that I can suggest is to keep those lines of communication open. If it's a matter of resentment, overwork, a sense of failure, stress, or distraction, he might finally come out and say it but not until he trusts you deeply with his heart.

You said, "Do I have a voice in this marriage, or am I supposed to be quiet and let him live the way he wants to live?" My answer would be to approach him with your requests but do so in love.

The Bible warns women about nagging, which tells us that this isn't anything new. Women have been nagging their husbands for thousands of years, but through the Word, God shows us that there is a better way to communicate. We should approach our husbands with love and humility—a hope that holds no expectation. And above all, be kind, tenderhearted, and willing to forgive. That's how you'll win his heart.

Looking to the Bible, we see a prime example in Esther, who approached the king (her husband) with honor and respect. She made her petition known and left it in his hands to make the decision.

Another example is Jesus, who lived in submission to the Father in heaven. Praying in the Garden of Gethsemane, He said, "Not my will, but thine, be done" (Luke 22:42).

Don't misunderstand the meaning of biblical submission. We *do* have a voice and an opinion. If we stifle our pain and our hurt we may grow to resent the men we once loved. When bitterness sets in, it takes root and will grow over time unless it is removed and replaced with something better. Be encouraged to share your thoughts, but hold back on the resentment if things don't go your way. Don't forget that God is in control and can change things at any time. Just do your part, and let God handle the rest.

Blessings,

Darlene

How do you treat a box that arrives at your door labeled "Fragile: Handle with Care"? When I see that, I make every effort not to shake up the contents, tip the box, or cut into it quickly. Wouldn't it be something if God stamped that message upon every person's heart? If He sent us into the world with a warning that read, "Handle this one with care"? Maybe we'd stop shaking things up as much as we do. Maybe we'd think twice before tipping scales in our favor. And perhaps we wouldn't be so quick to cut into people who hurt us. Maybe we'd handle their hearts with more care than we do.

Here's the thing. That's exactly what God has ordained us to do. Maybe it's not written on a sticker and slapped onto a box, but the message is every bit as clear: "Be ye kind one to another, tenderhearted, forgiving one another, even as God for Christ's sake hath forgiven you" (Eph. 4:32).

I didn't deserve Michael's love and forgiveness. I didn't deserve my family, and I didn't deserve to be loved by those whom I hurt. But in that moment of darkness when one person in this world cared enough to display the covenant-keeping love of Jesus Christ to His church, I turned from my sin and clung to the grace of God that is strong enough to break the bonds of sin and death.

"I'm sorry," he said.

Turning my head in disbelief, I looked over at my husband, who was weeping at the side of our bed. "What? What do *you* have to be sorry for?" I asked. My thoughts were swimming in shame and confusion.

"This isn't all *your* fault," he replied. "If I had only done things differently. If I had been more—"

"No," I sobbed, kneeling before him, "I won't let you take on my sin."

"Listen to me," Michael said, with tears streaming down his face. "I have a responsibility in this too."

I couldn't accept that, and I wouldn't. But still his words transformed me like nothing else ever had.

Forgiveness is one thing, but kind and tenderhearted

forgiveness is yet another. It excels the wisdom of man, reflecting the love of Christ.

In that moment of compassion and grace, I was reminded of our Savior, who said, "Neither do I condemn you; go and sin no more" (John 8:11 NKJV).

THE CHALLENGE

Practice communicating with your husband in love. Avoid the temptation to lash out in anger by keeping your tongue under control. No eye rolling, no stamping, and no raising your voice. Being gentle and patient might not come easily to you, but as with anything else, you will get better with practice.

| NINE |

Be the Woman Your Husband Needs You to Be

USUALLY, I GET UP WITH THE KIDS IN THE morning, we enjoy breakfast together, and I get them ready for school before taking a nap. This particular morning, however, Michael let me sleep in.

I'm pretty sure it had a lot to do with my bouncing around the house at 4:00 a.m. like a kitten with a new tennis ball. I had gone to bed early enough, but I just couldn't sleep.

When I can't sleep, I hop out of bed for any and every reason I can possibly think of. Did I turn the stove off? Is the back door unlocked? Did I charge the cell phone? Do I really have to tinkle again? Is that a hair that I feel on my chin?

Then my legs get choosy. One wants to be warm while the other is cool. I devise a plan to make both of them happy, by flipping one leg over the blankets. My back is cold, but not cold enough for a blanket, so I pull the top sheet up to my neck.

We have a king-sized bed, but since more than half of it is a waste we could probably make do with a twin. With pillows together, I squeeze in tight behind Michael's back where I can take in his scent. I swear there's no better smell on this earth except maybe a newborn—that just might be a tie.

After hours of tossing and turning and shifting and shuffling, Michael rolled over and finally asked, "You can't sleep?"

"No," I answered, "I've been wide awake for hours!" I let out a sigh.

"Turn off your alarm," he said. "I'll get up with the kids in the morning."

An invitation like that is one I take in a hurry.

At 8:00 a.m. I heard Michael rustling around in the bedroom. The jingling of change and the pace of his footsteps suggested he might need some attention.

"Is everything okay?" I asked.

"No," he answered, "I lost my keys." And with that he hurried out of the room and back down the stairs.

The bed was inviting. My legs had finally made up their minds, and my cool back had warmed up to the sheet. All I wanted to do was roll over and drift back to sleep, but I figured that getting up to find keys was a better idea.

A man without keys is like a woman experiencing PMS without chocolate. The entire house comes to a screeching halt until the problem is solved.

Putting on my robe, I hustled down the stairs where I found him tossing boots and shoes in the mudroom. By then he was running late. The kids decided to walk, but Michael had no choice. He couldn't leave without the keys. He had only two keys for the Jeep. One was lost, and the other was at work.

We spent the next hour retracing his steps, inspecting the sofa, sorting through trash, checking pockets, and searching through drawers. Anyplace that you can imagine, we thought of. We even tossed the bed twice.

We didn't find Michael's set of keys, but we did find three extra house keys, an *extra* Jeep key, a blue thumb ring, and a channel changer. All was not lost.

Standing in the kitchen, Michael lifted me onto the counter, held me around the waist, and leaned in. "Ugh. . . . Thank you," he said. "I can't believe how this morning is going."

He was able to get to his shop with the extra Jeep key we found, but once he got there things went from bad to worse. The employees were there to let him in, but his office door was still locked. The extra key to his office? It was inside his desk.

Hearing my husband tell me about how he climbed up a ladder and crawled through the ceiling to get over the wall got us both laughing so hard I was crying. I couldn't imagine my conservative husband with dress shirt and tie crawling anywhere, let alone through the ceiling at work. If laughter is medicine, we're both due for a healthy checkup, let me tell you!

By the way, the keys were in his jacket pocket—the very *first* place I told him to look, but he switched jackets the night before, and it slipped his mind. A morning like that reminds me of my created purpose in life, which is that of being his helper: "The LORD God said, It is not good that the man should be alone; I will make him an help meet for him" (Gen. 2:18). God could have populated this world exclusively with men, but He chose to create human beings who are perfectly suited, yet different from men in so many ways.

Michael could have looked for his keys alone, and he might have found them alone, but how much more comforting is it to have someone who walks alongside you? Someone to keep you warm at night, pick you up when you fall, help carry your burden, and remind you to laugh when life brings you down.

Have you ever realized that almost every living creature, including man, was created from the dust of this earth? The woman was the exception. The Bible makes a point of telling us this. Why? Because the woman was taken from the man so that she might return to that union as one with him.

Consider this verse, "Therefore shall a man leave his

father and his mother, and shall cleave unto his wife: and they shall be one flesh" (Gen. 2:24). Have you ever noticed that little word *cleave* tucked into this verse? And have you ever stopped to consider its significance? It means to keep, to stick with, and to hold close to, but there's also a deeper meaning.

A cleft is a split, a crack, or a division. We can look at cleaving this way: to divide along the natural grain forming a cleft is necessary when grafting two plants together. In order for those plants to survive this new union, they must be completely sealed.

When I consider this grafting of two plants, I can't help being reminded that God created Eve *from* Adam. When two are joined together in marriage, they return to their original state of union. A husband opens himself to envelop his bride, and the two grow together as one. When they are completely sealed by the Holy Spirit, that union is protected and strengthened. Like a cord of three strands, it's not easily broken.

Looking again at Genesis 2:18, we see the term *help meet*, which in the Hebrew text is *ezer kenegdo*. One scholar offers the translation as "sustainer beside him."[1] The word *ezer* is found several times throughout the Old Testament when describing *God* as our helper. But the fascinating part is that in nearly every reference where this term is used, God is coming to the rescue as He protects His people and defeats the enemy. One writer suggested, "A better translation . . . of *ezer* would be 'life-saver.' *Kenegdo* means alongside, or opposite to, a counterpart."[2]

How does that relate to my role as a wife? Reading these passages, I wonder whether my purpose in being a help meet runs deeper than doing the dishes, looking for keys, or folding his socks. Could it be that my purpose is to fight alongside my husband in battle? Could it be that my role as a help meet is to pray for him, encourage him in his walk of faith, and exemplify a strong faith of my own?

Don't get me wrong. Titus 2 calls women to be good keepers of their homes, so don't put down the duster just yet! But being a good keeper of the home includes watching over the affairs of your family—in other words guarding the castle from harm. What I suggest here is that we make a conscious effort to nurture our husbands spiritually through prayer and encouragement, so that we are the helpers that we were created to be.

Let's suit up for battle by putting on the armor of God in accordance with Ephesians 6. This verse stands out to me as I consider the ways in which our families come under attack: "Above all, taking the shield of faith, wherewith ye shall be able to quench all the fiery darts of the wicked" (Eph. 6:16). Our husbands, our children, and we ourselves are constantly faced with negative messages. When we stand strong in faith, we are prepared to quench each and every one with wisdom and strength from the Lord. This is why it's so important that we stand guard over our hearts and our loved ones.

The idea that you were created to be your husband's helper

is not popular in our modern culture. The moment you bring up this topic, the question of equality rises, and once again you're reminded that for the past forty years women have been fighting for *equal* rights and *equal* pay.

I'm not talking about *equality* here. It's clear in Scripture that Jesus had good relationships with women, just as He did with men, and He showed a great level of respect toward them. What I'm talking about is *identity*. When the two are confused, a problem arises. The lines between men and women are blurred while many in our society refuse to accept them as different.

In her book *The Female Brain*, Louann Brizendine, MD, wrote, "There are those who wish there were no differences between men and women. In the 1970s at the University of California, Berkeley, the buzzword among young women was 'mandatory unisex,' which meant that it was politically incorrect even to mention sex difference. There are still those who believe that for women to become equal, unisex must be the norm. The biological reality, however, is that there is no unisex brain."[3]

The Bible is rich with instruction on marriage as it outlines the roles of both husbands and wives. But when these roles don't make enough sense or make readers uncomfortable, they are often discarded, twisted, or ignored. Here's the thing. The Bible instructs believers to be set apart from this world, meaning *this age* or *this period of time*. In other words, we shouldn't conform to its standards just because it's the popular thing to do. If we say that we love God and seek His will for our lives, we have to be willing to follow His wisdom regardless of what popular opinions may be. God's commandments for marriage are every bit as fresh and relevant today as they were when He originally laid them out for us in Scripture.

The words *submission* and *help meet* are often paired together, and well they should be because both are commanded of wives in Scripture. The misconception, however, is that submission means women are less than men (here's that argument of equality again) and that this mind-set is old-fashioned and degrading to women.

The truth is that submission and equality are two different things. *Submission* is yielding your will for the good of another. It is putting another ahead of yourself. It's a choice that you make out of respect, love, and reverence. And for me it's a decision that's powered by faith. *Equality* of people refers to our value. We have equality among all men and women, yet some are in positions of authority over us, such as members of Congress, senators, and governors. They are in no way of greater value than the people they serve.

We see this pattern everywhere in our social system, but to get a better understanding of God's will for mankind, we have the infallible example of Jesus Christ found in Paul's letter to the Philippians: "Let this mind be in you, which was also in Christ Jesus: who, being in the form of God, thought it not robbery to be equal with God: but made himself of no reputation, and took upon him the form of a servant, and was made in the likeness of men: and being found in fashion as a man, he humbled himself, and became obedient unto death, even the death of the cross" (Phil. 2:5–8). With that scripture in mind, I understand that I'm in every way equal to my husband, but I shouldn't take advantage of equality for my own pleasure or gain. My desire is to please God by humbling myself and taking on the role of a help meet. If my Lord and Savior took on the role of a servant, why shouldn't I?

We were created by an almighty God who fashioned us to uniquely fit the desires of man. Because of that master design, we shouldn't let anyone say that our role as a wife is demeaning, undignified, or degrading. It's an honor to be sculpted by the Maker according to plan. Where men lack, we abound, and vice versa. No one can fill the role of a help meet like a woman can. You can never put two identical pieces of a puzzle together, but when you find one piece that fills the space that another one lacks, you start to see a bigger picture come to life.

Men and women are two very different beings. But in order to be politically correct, people accept that the lines of difference between a male and a female are blurred. Not only are the differences blurred, but pop culture encourages us to experiment with our sexuality while discouraging us from speaking out. It's time to speak out against this modern mind-set and to reclaim who we were created to be; after all we are the ones who are raising the next generation. If the lines are blurred, draw new ones. Be politically *incorrect* if you must, but count it an honor to be created a woman according to the perfect wisdom of God: "God created man in his own image, in the image of God created he him; male and female created he them" (Gen. 1:27).

Part of our role as wives is to offer emotional support to our husbands. We should be there to pick them up when life pulls them down and to cheer them on when the going gets tough. But there's so much more. Life is a spiritual war. Our husbands need us to ride beside them into battle anytime they come under attack. I'm prepared to meet my husband's needs *today*, but what if they change *tomorrow*? Will I be prepared?

It's easy for a marriage to thrive when conditions are good. Seriously, how bad can life be when our greatest stress is looking for keys? But what about those times when the going gets really tough? Stress, sickness, poverty, and death are realities for many families.

Michael and I never dreamed that we'd ever come to the place that we did. In fact we'd often remark about how we were the happiest couple in the world. And we were for a time. Nothing would ever come between us, or *so we thought*. But sin and temptation have a stronger pull on the heart than we realize, which is why we must stand strong against the enemy. We have to be ready at all times to fight for our marriages.

We never know what the future will bring. God does, which is why He allows our faith to be tried in hopes that we'll grow spiritually. He knows that in order for us to be prepared for *tomorrow*, we must be exercised by faith *today*.

If I just stopped there—discussing the role of a wife—we'd have much to think on and some good instruction for marriage, but we'd be missing out on a beautiful truth. We'd be overlooking the greatest part of creation and how it pertains to our purpose.

If you've ever wondered why God created this massive solar system that extends so far beyond our galaxy that astronomers couldn't possibly imagine its width or its depth; and if you ever questioned why in the midst of this ginormous creation He hung the earth, the moon, and the stars; if you wondered how and why He created man from the dust of the earth, the answer is simple: it's all for *His* pleasure. As John wrote, "Thou art worthy, O Lord, to receive glory and honour and power: for thou hast created all things, and for thy pleasure they are and were created" (Rev. 4:11). We weren't accidents, afterthoughts, or blips on His radar. We were created with the intent of bringing Him pleasure, and what truly brings God pleasure is obedience to His Word.

A happy marriage is not the goal; it is the inevitable fruit of a Christ-centered relationship. When a husband and a wife build a Christ-centered marriage where each is fulfilling his or her God-given role, they bring honor and glory to God.

THE CHALLENGE

Vigorous pursuit. That's my challenge for you. Take your eyes off the world and run into the arms of our Lord. Seek His will for your life. Search the Scriptures daily, and spend time with Him in prayer, asking that He guide you in your role as a wife. What does the Lord require of you? Listen for His voice, and when you hear it, forsake everything else to follow Him.

| TEN |

Be Affectionate in Ways That Are Pleasing to God

DO YOU REMEMBER THE FIRST TIME YOUR husband reached out for your hand? The first time his arm brushed up against yours? What about the day you shared your first kiss?

I remember ours.

We were standing on a rickety old footbridge next to the park where I grew up, looking down at the river. It was at least ten years since I had stood on that old bridge, and it was just as rundown as I had remembered. But there was something about it that drew me back time and again. Adventure perhaps? The wood was well aged, and a few of its planks were missing, which is probably what attracted us kids to it in the first place.

My sisters used to race their bicycles across it and wait for me on the other side, but I preferred to white knuckle the railing with a slow and steady walk. If I was going to die, it would be in a hospital bed near a bowl of cherry Jell-O, not plunging into the depths of the river below me. Can you call three feet of water "depths"? I guess when you're eight years old, you consider anything over two feet as deep water.

Fourteen years later, I was standing on the same bridge, looking at the same murky green water with Michael. Planks were still missing, and the wood wasn't getting any younger, but I felt safer than I ever had. I was standing at the edge of the world with my best friend, and there was no place on earth like it.

We had been friends for months already, spending much of the summer together, going on picnics, and taking long walks—nothing too serious. But that day was different. There was something in the air, and it wasn't the smell of algae.

Turning toward me, Michael leaned in, and for the first time his lips met mine. It was the kind of moment I had been dreaming about for years. Everything about it was perfect, including and especially the man I was with.

To this day I love the sights and sounds of the riverbank. Just last summer we took our kids there to show them the bridge and reminisce about the old days. Unfortunately, the wood has been replaced by much sturdier concrete, but the riverbank is the same way we left it—a stagnant but beautiful murky green.

I also remember the first time we held hands. His arm often brushed up against mine when we were sitting in church or taking a walk in the park. It was usually just a slight touch, but it was enough to put my stomach in knots and get the butterflies moving. Every look and every touch went straight to my heart, but nothing compared to that moment when his fingers finally slipped into mine. Two puzzle pieces fitting together as one.

The stars were aglow. The summer air swept through, washing over us with a fresh breeze from the lake, and the two of us walked hand in hand. The touch of his skin brought a new dimension to our relationship; perhaps one could call it the "language" of touch. And maybe we should. After all, one touch can say more in a single moment than our words ever could. After twenty-five years I can say without a doubt that we continue to speak this language and to learn as each year goes by.

I can't imagine any relationship thriving without touch any more than I could imagine two people living in a house where they never communicated a single thought to each other. How sad would that be? We hear plenty about the importance of communication, and we should because it's a vital part of any growing relationship. But what we don't hear enough about is the importance of touch and how it plays a vital part in bonding two people together.

If you're a mother, you'll likely remember the first moments spent with your newborn. We have a natural desire to hold them during those first years of bonding. As they grow to the point where they are crawling and walking, we must continue to offer them physical contact. It may be in the way that we hug our children, hold hands with them, or offer a gentle pat on the back.

I remember when my son Graham was born. He's one of those babies who, like many others, suffered from jaundice. His bilirubin count was off the charts. All my babies had it, but Graham definitely suffered the most. He was always the sick one. They placed him in a glass box that resembled a fish tank, and for several days our little one remained there under the lights. In order to protect his eyes, they glued Velcro to the sides of his face and put a little blindfold on him. The tank had circles cut out of the side wall so we parents could put our hands in and massage the baby while he slept. I'd often stand at the side of Graham's tank, rubbing his little back or holding his hand just so he'd know I was there, but nothing compared to the skin-to-skin contact we had when he was out of the tank. Just being able to hold him while he ate was a necessary part of the bonding process for both of us.

Let's stop and consider this: if our physical touch and affection nourish growing children and are necessary to the bonding process, imagine the nourishment and bonding they bring to a growing relationship between a husband and a wife.

Here's an excerpt from an article I came across by Benedict Carey discussing the effects of physical touch and its benefit to team sports:

> To see whether a rich vocabulary of supportive touch is in fact related to performance, scientists at Berkeley recently analyzed interactions in one of the most physically expressive arenas on earth: professional basketball. Michael W. Kraus led a research team that coded every bump, hug and high five in a single game played by each team in the National Basketball Association early last season.
>
> In a paper due out this year in the journal *Emotion*, Mr. Kraus and his co-authors, Cassy Huang and Dr. Keltner, report that with a few exceptions, good teams tended to be touchier than bad ones.[1]

Carey went on to say—and this is my favorite part of the study—that the part of the brain that solves problems responds to touch, sending it a message of relaxation. He wrote, "In effect, the body interprets a supportive touch as 'I'll share the load.'"[2]

Isn't that what being a couple is all about? Sharing the load, being there to support and encourage each other. We can see from the study that touch can be as simple as a high five, but maybe a hug would translate better between a husband and a wife.

I wasn't always a hugger, and we weren't much of a hugging family when I was growing up. I remember leaning in and kissing my mom on the cheek every night before bed, but other than that we didn't touch all that much.

Until I got married.

Michael's grandma was a hugger, so marrying into his family meant that I'd soon be one, too—whether I liked it or not. At first it felt a little invasive to me, to be honest. After all, I wasn't used to having anyone step into my space other than Michael. I imagine that I was probably one of the stiffest huggers they'd ever encountered, but I soon got used to it, and after a while I got to like it a lot. All thanks to Gram.

After a while I carried this little habit over to my parents' house, embracing them as often as I could. And when we found out that my dad was sick with cancer, I wouldn't leave their house without kissing him and giving them both a big hug.

When you see that you're losing someone, you suddenly realize that every minute you have with him or her is a gift from God. Every hug, every word, every kiss—all gifts that I tucked into the treasure chest of my heart. I cherished his wisdom, his loving-kindness, and yes, especially his touch.

We all need physical contact. Studies have proved that, and common sense confirms it to be true. So the only question that remains is, are we hugging and touching enough? Are we kissing our husbands as much as we could be? Are we holding hands like we used to? And finally are we hugging them with intent? A hug should not only remind them of how much we love them; it should signify that we're right where we want to be.

One hug from Michael tells me that I'm secure in his arms. I can go from feeling completely frazzled and frustrated to a feeling of peace and serenity in a matter of minutes. When he leans in and holds me close to his heart, there's nothing quite like it. During those moments I'm thankful for his broad shoulders, rock-hard chest, and strong arms. It's a comforting place to be. His masculinity is more than something I *want*; it's something I *crave* as a woman. It's not a coincidence that God created men one way and women another.

If we go back to the symbolism of marriage and how it reflects the relationship between Jesus Christ and the church, we see a picture of God as our protector, reminding us of the protection a husband offers his wife: "He shall cover thee with his feathers, and under his wings shalt thou trust: his truth shall be thy shield and buckler" (Ps. 91:4).

God in all His wisdom created men and women so differently. I can only imagine how Michael feels in my arms and how he reacts to my softer, feminine touch. Whether we're kissing, hugging, making love, or simply holding hands as we walk, we're speaking a language that's louder than words, and one that should not be tuned out.

If you're newly married, you might be wondering why you're

reading this chapter. Most newlyweds can't keep their hands off each other, so why would you need a chapter on touching?

When I was a teenager, our pastor gave us an illustration. He said that if a newlywed couple kept a jar beside their bed and put a penny in it each time they made love, they'd fill it up in the first year. But if for the rest of their lives, they took a penny out each time they made love, they'd never empty the jar. I don't know how accurate that is, but I see the point he was making. Couples tend to get so busy with life that they often forget that they're lovers. Even worse than that are spouses who stop touching each other altogether. If you are newly married, you need to be aware of how quickly it can slip away when you don't cherish the importance of touch.

Michael and I have never stopped being physical with each other, but there was a time when things became little more than routine. The more that resentment built up between us, the less we were lovers. And the less we were lovers, the more we resented each other.

It's important to see the difference here. Sex for the sake of having sex isn't the same as making love with your husband. When a husband and a wife make love, they are engaged in the moment. They tune out the world around them and tune in to each other.

Forget about what you're making for dinner tomorrow, what one friend said to the other, or what color drapes you want for the nursery, and allow yourself to be in the moment.

If you're too busy to make love to your husband, you're busier than God ever intended you to be. Slow down, enjoy this time together, and don't let this area of your marriage slip away from you. If you're not touching the people that you love, you're missing out on an entirely deeper level of communication.

There are probably a dozen more reasons that a couple should touch, but I'd like to share five of the primary reasons that stand out to me:

1. It promotes bonding between two people.
2. It reminds a person that he or she is loved.
3. It reinforces security in a marriage.
4. It fills up the love tank.
5. It energizes another.

Many couples stop speaking the language of touch because they aren't making it a priority. Perhaps a better way to put this would be that they aren't making their *spouses* a priority.

Naturally, there will be seasons of your life when you are too exhausted at the end of a day to even feel sexy, never mind *be* sexy, such as when you are nursing an infant or raising several young children. That's understandable. Young children can be exhausting. There's no doubt about it. I've been there, and I remember it well. I barely had time to take a shower, and when I finally did take one, I knew that I'd be sacrificing any chance for a nap. If I did try to nap, it rarely worked in my favor. By the time I was relaxed enough to nod off to sleep, the baby would be finished with his nap and start fussing again.

Depending on the season of your life, your love life may slow down a bit. But keep in mind that slowing down and *eliminating* it are two different things. Never ignore it, and don't place it on the back shelf where you forget about it. Just like anything else that's a priority in your life, you may need to examine your schedule to see what you can cut and what you must keep. Sex aside here, regardless of how busy you are or how exhausted you might be, don't stop holding, hugging, and kissing your spouse. It really doesn't take any energy to cuddle together on the couch, does it?

Here's a peek into my life. This afternoon while Michael was out running errands, I decided to take a little nap. The minute he got home and walked through the door, I heard his footsteps coming up the stairs to find me (he does this every single time he comes home). And every time I hear the door open, I drop what I'm doing and embrace him with a hug and a kiss. It's my way of showing Michael that he's important to me. It's really a beautiful thing to see him walk through the door after work. Our two birds start chirping, the pugs run to the door with their tails wagging, and the kids gather around while I give him a hug and a kiss. It's like a minicelebration of our day.

It's okay to have a routine like Michael and I do. But don't let that routine become boring. Don't fall into the habit of rambling off the same few words every day while you give him a quick peck on the lips. Be present in the moment. Say something meaningful, and hug with intention.

I'm most responsive to Michael when he says something unexpected. He tells me that he loves me and that he's proud of me all the time—at least once a day. But when he says something out of the blue like, "You're an incredible mom," or "You're one of the strongest people I know," my brain flips a switch and the words sink in. Those are the thoughts that I turn over in my brain and think about for a while. And of course, I have the same reaction when it comes to his touch. I'm used to getting a hug when he walks in the door or when he's heading off to bed, and I like it, but the unexpected hugs and kisses are the ones that tend to sink in the most.

All marriages are different, all our circumstances are different, and all our husbands are different. The important thing is that we're willing to give our best to our marriages according to the will of God.

On that note, I'm reminded of a conversation with a friend this afternoon. Another friend of ours—a writing friend—encouraged her readers to give their comfy nightgowns the night off and put on something sexy to please their husbands. Some readers were in favor of the idea, while others were opposed to it, saying that while we are in the world, we should not be of it—pretty yes, trashy no. So is it a sin to wear sexy lingerie, or is it okay within the boundaries of marriage? In particular, a *Christian* marriage.

I was able to share this letter that I received from a reader, which is good food for thought:

Dear Darlene,

I have a personal question to ask you.

I'm engaged to be married to a man who is a strong man of God. That's what attracted me to him in the first place and what continues to capture my heart. He's loyal to me and our Savior. And I know that I can safely trust him with my heart.

Unlike most guys his age, he's a man of prayer and purity. We have both saved ourselves for marriage because our purity is a gift we have reserved for each other.

I read a lot of Christian blogs, and they seem to differ in opinion when it comes to the subject of intimate clothing. Some say that it's a sin to wear sexy lingerie, while others (Christian writers) say that we should be dressing provocatively for our husbands.

So my question is, once we are married, how should I dress for my husband? Specifically, how should I dress for him when we are alone in the bedroom?

I want to dress to please my husband, but I don't want to lead him away from the Lord.

Bride in Training

Dear Bride in Training,

I've decided to turn to my husband for his thoughts on this because your fiancé sounds much like Michael in so many ways. I'm thankful I did because his wisdom runs deep.

Michael is a godly man whose sole purpose in life is serving God. In fact he wakes an hour earlier every day (5:00 a.m.) just so he can spend that time with God. Serving God is his focus, and seeing women on billboards or at the office dressed in low-cut lingerie doesn't entice him—it annoys him and reminds him of how corrupt our world has become. When he comes home, he desires to see something different—a wife who glorifies God. He wants sex to be a beautiful experience that expresses our love, not one's release of pent-up lust from a long day's work with enticing women.

Do I think that sexy lingerie in the bedroom between a husband and a wife is wrong? Absolutely not. If it appeals to you both and you are comfortable with it, by all means wear it to please your husband.

My point is this: don't measure your standard by the standard of the world; measure it against your relationship and what brings honor and respect to your marriage. Dressing in a provocative way might be confusing for both of you, so I'd start by wearing feminine nightgowns that remind him you're a woman, then after time you will start to learn his preferences, and if you are comfortable, dress accordingly.

Our biggest battle is that the world constantly inundates us. We need not conform to its standards. We are conforming to biblical standards. The Bible isn't specific about this topic but reminds us that conscience will be our guide. Therefore, whatever choices we make should honor both God and our marriages.

Remember what Paul wrote: "I beseech you therefore, brethren, by the mercies of God, that ye present your bodies a living sacrifice, holy, acceptable unto God, which is your reasonable service. And be not conformed to this world: but be ye transformed by the renewing of your mind, that ye may prove what is that good, and acceptable, and perfect, will of God" (Rom. 12:1–2).

Blessings,
Darlene

THE CHALLENGE

Consider ways to be affectionate with your husband that you might usually overlook. Don't smother him, but seize opportunities as they arise. Hold hands while you're shopping, sit beside him on the sofa at home, put a hand on his shoulder when you ask him a question, slip a love note into his lunch, hug him when he walks in the door, or rub his back at night.

Be creative. Every marriage is different; you're the best judge when it comes to deciding when and what he might like.

ELEVEN

Seize the Day and Capture the Joy

MY TUMMY WASN'T FEELING WELL, BUT I figured the discomfort would soon work itself out. It could have been the pasta salad or the venti mocha with extra whip that was a surprise from Michael, but more likely it was the Jolly Rancher candies I had been consuming by the truckload. That had to be it.

My daughter, Madison, and I had recently discovered a mutual attraction to the candy. I'm not usually one to eat sugar, but those little babies had me fiercely in their grip. One after the other, I was popping them in, enjoying every single minute of the tangy, sweet flavor. Madison likes the purple ones, but I'm more of a blue raspberry girl, which balances things out quite nicely until we're all out of choices and both of us go for the green.

Yeah, it must be the candy.

With every minute I felt a little worse until I started to feel far worse than I ever had. First I loosened my belt and then my jeans, but nothing made a difference. The pain was so excruciating that I was barely able to walk. Every breath was more painful than the last. On a scale of one to ten with one being a pimple and ten giving birth to quadruplets, this pain was holding firm at nine.

I made my way upstairs to where Michael was sleeping and somehow dragged myself, moaning and groaning in pain, over to his side of the bed. Normally, I'd let him sleep through and deal with a tummy ache alone, but this one was different. I wasn't sure if my stomach was about to explode, and I didn't want to be alone if it did.

For the next three hours he stayed by my side, gently rubbing my back and coaching me to relax. His voice was gentle and strong. "Just breathe," he said.

Nothing was more comforting than knowing that I wasn't alone as I listened to the soothing sound of his voice.

It's not every day that I appreciate Michael like that. I do for the most part, but there are some days when his actions get under my skin. When he's had a crazy, stressful day that turns into a stressful week and everything starts to bother him, then it starts to bother me too. The dog is too naughty, he can't find his tie, and he examines every spoon he pulls from the drawer and throws it in the sink. Days like that tend to make me forget how soothing his voice is and how comforting his presence can be. There's nothing quite like it. But I do forget because my view of him is so clouded by stress.

On days like that I have to remind myself that I'm in love with a soul who is clothed in human flesh with the weight of the world heavy upon his shoulders. What would I do without him? Without those shoulders to lean on? I can't imagine it for a minute, but doing so reminds me of how marriage is a gift that's nothing short of incredible. So precious, yet so often tossed to the side.

To think that I came so close to losing him. How did I ever get to the place where I took him for granted? How could I have possibly forgotten the joy we once shared and who he was to my heart? I held a gem of great worth in the palm of my hand, and I was willing to trade it for a counterfeit coin.

What does it take to wake us up and make us realize what we have? If only we could all see the beauty of love before it slips away from our grasp.

I cohosted an online marriage series called "Revive Your Marriage." It was a month-long challenge that encouraged women in different areas of their marriages. In response to the series, one participant, Nicole, posted an article on her blog along with this question: "If one day he didn't come home, would I have to live with regrets of how or what I did (or didn't do) for him?"

Just three months later she wrote, "I'm not even sure that I have the words to say this. . . . On Thursday, December 13th, I received a phone call that forever altered my life. I got a call from my husband's business partner saying that a tree had fallen on him while he was working. I hurried down to the job only to find that he was already with Jesus."

A sobering thought, isn't it? I was devastated when I read that. It could have been me; it could have been you; it could have been any one of us.

Life is too short to take our loved ones for granted, and Nicole realized that *before* he was gone. I asked her if I could publish her article that she wrote just three months before her husband, Chad, went to be with the Lord.

What if You Didn't Have "One More Time"?

This is a topic near and dear to my heart. I could have easily lost my hubby to a work accident a little over a year into our marriage. While that opened my eyes to how short life can be, I still fell back into a pattern of selfishness after he healed. We had some very hard years following that time. It always fell back to finances, which were frequently non-existent. We were aware that our fights almost always fell back to a money issue, but I think I also liked to fight because I had this insatiable desire to be right (and be in control).

My need to be in control (of everything) was causing me to base my treatment of my hubby on works (what he did for me or how he treated me). I'm not even sure when it hit me, but one day I had a realization.

If one day he didn't come home, would I have to live with regrets of how or what I did (or didn't do) for him?

For example:

+ Would getting up to pack his lunch be a big deal?
+ Would I long to rub his back . . . just one more time? (He has back issues due to the accident, and I too often gripe about this never-ending task.)
+ Would I find the energy to "have fun in the bedroom" . . . just one more time?
+ Would I drop what I was doing to help him with whatever . . . just one more time?

I have to be careful because these thoughts can cause me to fall into a state of constant worry that something will, indeed, happen to him . . . but keeping this perspective has taken so much of the laziness or irritation that some-times pops up at bay.

I cringe when I hear women griping about having to do this or that for their hubby. I just think, "What if he wasn't here. What would you give to be able to do that for him one more time?"

I used to get so mad when my hubby didn't act how I wanted him to or do what I wanted him to, but when you are just thankful for one more day with him; it makes the little things seem so unimportant.

Yes, I still occasionally whine about rubbing his back. I still grumble to myself when I pick his dirty clothes up off the floor or put his dog collar chargers away (for the millionth time) . . . but in my mind I constantly hear "be thankful for this stuff to do because it means he's still here with you."

Perspective is everything!

There will always be things that bug you about your spouse, but in their absence . . . would those things actu-ally be that bad? [1]

Those words certainly put things in perspective for me. No, we don't love our husbands merely because life is short and they might not be here tomorrow. We love them because we are committed to glorifying God in our marriages. But the reality is still there—life is too short to take anything for granted.

Marriage isn't a dress rehearsal for the big show. This *is* the show, and every line that we deliver dictates how the story will go. We have the choice to either sit around waiting for life to be everything that we hoped it would be or start making this life—the moment we're in right now—a wonderful place. We can't see today as a gift until we lift our eyes to the Giver. But the moment that we do stop in the midst of this busy world to give thanks, we see beauty.

Have you ever left something on the floor of your home, like a basket of clothes? And after stepping over it so many times you started to forget it was there? Maybe you haven't—more than likely you're a better housekeeper than I am—but I have. One day my daughter put a basket of clothes at the top of the stairs just outside my bedroom door. Several days passed before I stopped and said, "Oh, that's where that purple sweater is!"

Unfortunately, we can be the same way with the people in our lives. Going about our work, day after day, we get so used to hurrying by that we forget to stop and breathe in the life around us and the people that God has given us.

The world is alive when we open our eyes to it. When we stop long enough to give thanks for what we *have* instead of complaining about what we *don't have*, we're able to breathe in the sweet scent of His blessings.

I tend to remember this most during the quiet hours of the night. After the kids go to bed, I get this sudden urge to sneak into their rooms and kiss their foreheads. And when Michael's asleep, I snuggle up close to his pillow where I can smell him too. I've actually gotten used to his snoring, and most days I kind of like it because it reminds me that I'm not alone in the dark.

It's surprising to discover all the little gifts you enjoy when you actually stop to consider them, isn't it?

It's natural to appreciate my husband when everything is going my way. It's easy when things are coming together, and he's going along with the flow. That's when I usually start counting my blessings and telling myself what an incredible husband I have.

It's not so easy on the days when *my* idea of how things should be done conflict with *his*. When things aren't coming together the way that I hoped they would. On such days I'm not counting my blessings too quickly because I'm too busy counting my wants, my needs, and my desires.

Whenever I'm in the zone of self-centered desire and pride, I hear a voice that beckons me without fail to let go of my selfish behavior. I'm offered a choice. Either I can be thankful to God in the moment, or I can hang on to my anger and make everyone around me miserable too. Thankfully, I'm learning that the moment I let go of my anger and humble myself before God, I find joy and peace that I would otherwise miss.

Believe me, it still happens. Just last night, we had planned to have a game night with the kids. After dinner was finished, the plates were washed, and we were ready to sit down and play, Michael decided to hit the treadmill first so he could get that out of the way.

Really? I thought. Nathaniel goes to bed at 9:00, and it was already 6:30. I wasn't impressed with that idea at all!

By the time he completed his ninety-minute workout and shower, I had lost my zeal for the one-hour game night. In other words, I was pouting. I told him that I was too tired to play and that I had some writing to do, which was true, but the bigger truth was that I was angry because things weren't going my way. Perhaps I had a right to be angry. But I also had a choice, and I made the wrong one.

Recall this popular passage: "Wherefore comfort yourselves together, and edify one another, even as also ye do . . . See that none render evil for evil unto any man; but ever follow that which is good, both among yourselves, and to all men. Rejoice evermore. Pray without ceasing. In every thing give thanks: for this is the will of God in Christ Jesus concerning you" (1 Thess. 5:11, 15–18). You might have applied it to the stressful situations in your life. Good. But have you ever considered that passage to be a vital ingredient for marriage? Being vigilant in the faith while edifying each other in love, striving for peace, and yes—giving thanks in good times *and bad.*

Although I should have communicated my frustration in love to Michael, I also should have chosen to be thankful to God for the time that we did have. I should have embraced the moment with joy instead of choosing to wallow in darkness.

Being thankful when you're not *feeling* it is a way of showing God that you trust Him to handle the situation. It's a way of showing Him that you're willing to let go of your anger and frustration and turn the wheel over to Him. It's also a way to exercise patience by trading instant gratification for long-term fulfillment.

The problem with most marriages today is that couples aren't willing to trust God for their futures or walk the sacrificial path that leads to a deeper commitment. People want happiness, and they want it *now*!

The sad thing about happiness is that it's fleeting. Things make us happy, people make us happy, and easy relationships make us happy. For a time. The moment our circumstances change, people disappoint us, or the relationship gets tough, we're right back where we started—unhappy.

Joy and peace are quite different. Consider the life of Mother Teresa. She was a missionary for more than forty-five years with a vow to give wholeheartedly to the poor. Rather than opt for a comfy life, she chose a life of poverty, saying, "As to my calling, I belong to the world. As to my heart, I belong entirely to the Heart of Jesus."[2] I love that, don't you?

This same woman who suffered much for the people collaborated on the book *The Joy in Loving: A Guide to Daily Living.* She found joy in the midst of poverty and pain because joy doesn't depend on our surroundings. It springs up from within and moves its way out.

I'm not suggesting that you choose a life of poverty and pain (unless God calls you to it, of course). I am suggesting that wherever you are in your marriage, you choose to appreciate what you have today. You might not be out on a mission field feeding the poor, but if you've picked up this book, I'm guessing that you have a mission at home—to be the best wife that God has called you to be.

This evening I sat down with a friend. I admire her love for Jesus and can sense her undeniable joy. You'd love her too. She's a joyful little thing with a bouncy ponytail and a spirit to match. I have yet to see this woman having a bad day.

I asked, "Bev, why do you think it's so important that we pursue Christ in our lives?"

I loved her answer.

"Because God wants us to experience a small part of heaven here and now. Life isn't just about the fact that we're going to heaven 'someday,'" she said. "He wants to indwell us *today* and shine in us now!"

Hallelujah, I'll have what she's living! Don't you love it when friends sharpen you like that?

Most marriages are about who we are as a couple, not

who we are in Christ. But when we live in a Christ-centered relationship, we walk in the light of beautiful love. It's popular these days for women to step out of their marriages on a mission to "find themselves," like a channel changer that's been lost in the sofa for years. But why are they lost in the first place?

The next time you're standing in line at the supermarket, take a look at the magazine covers, especially the headlines. The words that pop up most often are *you, your, have, get, enjoy,* and *yourself.* See a pattern there?

We're naturally self-centered, and when we give in to that self-centered attitude, we're on a never-ending quest for more of what makes us happy. Those who are Christ-centered live from the inside out. Their joy comes from the Lord, and they seek to please others.

Reading Nicole's words, I was blown away by the fact that God's hand was upon her months before Chad's passing. She wrote, "In my mind I constantly hear 'be thankful for this stuff to do because it means he's still here with you.'"

Not many of us get that kind of heart preparation. Or maybe we do, and we just don't listen to the voice. If you did have that undeniable feeling that your husband might not be there tomorrow, what would you change? Stop and think about that a minute. What would you change today, and what would you miss tomorrow? Ralph Waldo Emerson encouraged us to "never lose an opportunity of seeing anything that is beautiful; for beauty is God's handwriting."[3]

THE CHALLENGE

The blessings we take for granted are gifts from the heart of a compassionate God who knows us intimately and cares for us deeply. Gifts can be anything from the smell of a newborn's skin to the way that your husband smiles at you. Each and every blessing has been handcrafted by the Creator Himself. Get a little notebook, and start keeping a gratitude journal. Then take a few minutes out of each day to record your many blessings.

TWELVE

Build a Strong Friendship

It was November 2, 1972.

Mom was at home unpacking our things, Dad was at work making concrete bricks, and I was settling into my new school. Not just *any* new school, this one had an underground tunnel, an old bell tower, and a fire escape that was more like a spiral slide.

Mrs. Spear was the first person I met. Her thin stature, sharp features, and horn-rimmed glasses told me that she was about 125 years old. Crooked finger pointing toward an empty desk, she motioned me to take a seat near the front of the class.

To my right side was a chubby brunette named Debbie, who spent most days behind her inhaler. She had asthma—nothing more—but since I didn't know much about the disease, it terrified me. I wondered how she got in bed at night and if her parents carried her through the house to eat meals and take baths. Surely she didn't walk on her own.

To my left was a skinny little girl named Woodrow, who was barely wider than a teaspoon. Turning in her chair, Woodrow peered over thick lenses, watching as I took my seat. Her brown hair was tousled about like she had slept on it wet. Her face was pale, her eyes were dark, and her lips were licorice red. She didn't smile much—at least not that day.

Looking down at my desk, I could sense that the other kids were staring at me, too, and while I felt the heat rise in my face, I wondered whether they'd figure out just how scared I was. I had left my friends and the only school I had ever known behind. Everything was new to me: the house, the children, the teachers. I wondered how long it would take until things felt like *home* again.

"Pull out your crayons," Mrs. Spear said, drawing attention to the front of the class. "Danny, can you pass out these papers?"

Reaching into my desk, I pulled out an eight-pack of crayons and waited while Danny passed me a paper. I'd later come to know him as Danny Hart, the boy whose challenge was to make me as miserable as he possibly could for the next eight years. The only upside was that his name rhymed with *fart*, and the other kids never let him forget it.

Just as I was about to start coloring, I noticed Woodrow. She was holding the fattest crayon I'd ever seen in my life, and all I could think of was that the crayon was almost as thick as her arm. With elbows out and chin held close to the page, she started coloring, unaware of the fact that I thought that she was a curious girl.

After more coloring, a few stories, and an interesting song about whooping cough, the lunch bell finally rang. Unlike my last school where we had a cloakroom at the back of the class, the kids hustled into the hallway to pick up their jackets and boots. I followed suit.

It's funny how you can stand in a crowded room full of people and still feel alone, isn't it? Children were flooding into the hallway, and I stood there alone. Not one face familiar to me. Not one friend to talk with.

My stomach was growling, and I got to wondering what Mom would be making for lunch. It was always a surprise, and it was *always* something good. Whether it was pizza on a bun, tomato and macaroni soup, or chicken noodle soup and bologna sandwiches, I was pleasantly surprised every time.

Just then I felt a tap on my back. "Hi," a cheerful tone caught my attention, "I'm Margo."

I turned around to see a blonde girl with a pixie-cut hairdo, a small mouth, and sparkling blue eyes. "Do you want to be my best friend?" she asked.

I had never met this girl before, hadn't even noticed her

sitting in class, but I was thrilled at the opportunity of having a new friend. Not just any new friend—a "best" friend.

It happened much sooner than I imagined it would, but standing in that hallway of my new school, I felt like I was finally *home*. Someone in this world noticed me and cared enough to reach out a hand of friendship that told me I wasn't alone.

For the next six years Margo and I were inseparable. Attached at the hip, we spent every day hanging out. Whether we were having lunch at school, running through the riverbanks, or enjoying hot days at the pool, we were closer than two friends could be. We spent time together, we kept each other's secrets, and we had each other's back.

Have you ever had a close friend like that? One that you could confide in, run to, and laugh with? If you're a woman, my guess is that you probably have at some point in your life, and you just might have one now. There's nothing quite like it, is there? That kind of friend doesn't come around every day, and when he or she does, you just know it's a *God* thing.

The blessings of having a best friend are many:

+ He has your back.
+ He is there when you run to him with your ups and your downs.
+ He reminds you that you're wanted and loved.
+ He knows how to cheer you up when you're down.
+ He can make you laugh like no one else can.

+ He is honest with you in a gentle and compassionate way.
+ He can be trusted with your emotions.
+ He allows you to be yourself.
+ He is a personal cheerleader who wants the best for you.
+ He encourages your personal growth.

I've had a few best friends over the course of my lifetime—friends who have made me laugh until I cried, friends I've made long-lasting memories with, and friends I could count on to encourage me when life got me down. They were definitely in my corner and reminded me how much I was loved. But I have to tell you, none of them will ever compare to Michael.

A best friend is a God thing, especially when that best friend is your husband. Friendship is the jelly in the sandwich of marriage. It holds you together on the days when life pulls the plate out from under you. I've had a few days like that. I think we all have. You know those days when all you want to do is stay in bed and pull the covers up over your head? Yeah, me too. When times of stress hit me, I quietly slip away, sneak up to my bedroom, and crawl under the covers. I find a sense of comfort there. A blanket is my shield from the world.

After all these years, Michael's gotten to know me well enough to detect when I'm upset or when I'm just taking a nap. Not two minutes after I crawl into bed, I hear the squeak of the door hinge followed by the shuffle of footsteps. "Okay," he'll say, sitting on the edge of the bed. "What's up?"

My standard response is usually, "I don't know," while I sink deeper into the blankets.

And then he'll gently pull the blanket back and encourage me to connect. "C'mon, I'm not leaving until we talk about what's going on."

A good friend finds you in the dark and carries you back to the light. At least that's what Michael does again and again. He's not only there when I seek him; he pursues me when I need him the most.

There are many ways to capture the heart of your husband, but if you want to capture his heart for a lifetime, work on being his *friend*. Be that person who makes him laugh and cheers him on. Assure him that he can trust his heart with you, and remind him how much you love him.

Let's look a little closer at love and friendship: "The aged women likewise, that they be in behaviour as becometh holiness, not false accusers, not given to much wine, teachers of good things; that they may teach the young women to be sober, to love their husbands, to love their children" (Titus 2:3–4). In the phrase "to love their husbands" the Greek word for "love" is *phileo*, meaning to be friends or to be friendly to someone.

The English language is complicated, and it is sometimes confusing for those of us who are English speakers. I can't imagine the confusion that it must cause those who speak other languages and are trying to learn it. For example, we have one word for love: I can love my husband and love a cheeseburger at

BUILD A STRONG FRIENDSHIP

the same time. The Greeks, on the other hand, have more clarity in their language. When they're talking about love, they spell it out clearly using one of several words. Here are four of them:

> *Agape* is sacrificial love, like the one we read about in
> 1 Corinthians 13.
> *Eros* is passionate love, the kind that makes your heart
> race.
> *Phileo* is friendship or affection.
> *Storge* is affection, usually within family relationships.

While a good marriage should have all four of these characteristics of love working together, the one that's at the heartbeat of marriage is *phileo*—friendship.

Remember that marriage is a reflection of the covenant between Jesus Christ and the church, and what He wants from the church, aside from our obedience to His Word, is our *fellowship*. He referred to believers as His friends (John 15), and He also said, "Behold, I stand at the door, and knock: if any man hear my voice, and open the door, I will come in to him, and will sup with him, and he with me" (Rev. 3:20).

What do we see happening in the church today? In too many cases people attend service on Sundays, pay their tithes, and do their best not to swear, but they don't have a personal *relationship* with the Lord. I'm not judging their hearts. All I am saying is that there's a priceless relationship that shouldn't be overlooked. When Michael pursues me—when he finds me in the dark and carries me back to the light—he reflects the love of our Savior, who desires to be our most intimate friend.

When He's nothing but a ticket to heaven or a "Get Out of Hell Free" card, the element of friendship is lost. Sure, a level of sacrifice might be taking place, but in many cases, *friendship* with God is nonexistent.

In the same way, we see housewives who cook, clean, keep their whites white, and drive kids to soccer on Saturdays, but they've forgotten what it is like to be friends with their husbands.

When God created Adam, He saw that man was alone. Adam needed someone to spend time with, someone he could confide in, someone he could laugh with, someone who was loyal to him, someone who would value him, and someone who would show him affection. God saw that he needed a companion and friend. God created Eve to be Adam's helper, but she was also God's gift of friendship to man, just as we are gifts of friendship to our husbands.

We find another kind of friendship in Scripture described in the story of David and Jonathan. They were holy men devoted to serving God, and their lives provide an incredible testimony of friendship and loyalty. Their souls were knit together as one (1 Sam. 18:1). It doesn't get much better than that, does it?

But here's the thing: the beauty of their friendship wasn't

based on their going to football games together or shooting the breeze at Starbucks. All that is fun, and they probably did have some guy time, but what speaks to us most about Jonathan is that he had David's back. He was loyal.

Just to give you a little background, the complete story is in 1 Samuel 18–23. After David was anointed to be the next king, King Saul took him into his household, made him a commander of the army, and gave him a daughter in marriage. Yet jealousy and anger so overtook Saul that he was desperate to have David killed. He attempted it several times, but each time David escaped.

With the help of Jonathan, the king's own son, David fled to the wilderness and went into hiding. Their parting words were, "May the LORD be between you and me, and between your descendants and my descendants, forever" (1 Sam. 20:42 NKJV).

Although Jonathan was the son of a king, he lived in submission to David. He was aware of and obedient to the fact that David was an anointed servant of the Lord. When he humbled himself by turning away from his own family to protect David's life, he was giving up any chance at being established as the next king. Nevertheless, Jonathan wanted the best for his friend. Their friendship was sealed with a covenant that was to be kept between them and their descendants forever.

This story illustrates that true friendship is not self-seeking. If we want to strengthen the bond, we must be willing to give up our desires for the good of another.

I've heard it said, "I love my husband, but I don't like him." Although that might sound like a deep thought with philosophical meaning, it makes me shake my head and say, "Okay—what?" It's kind of like saying she's pregnant, but she's not. The two don't mix. If you really love something, you won't have any problem saying that you like it, and you won't have any problem telling the world just how much. What she might really be trying to say is, "I love my husband, but our friendship has faded away." Maybe the two have drifted apart. That would make sense.

The truth is that many couples have forgotten how to be friends over time. They don't even know what that relationship looks like anymore. And the sad thing is, they don't know how to bring it back. The idea is to start working on *your* heart before you attempt to change *his*. Think about a good friend you've had over the years, and list the qualities that defined your friendship. What made that friendship strong? What set it apart? If you want to rekindle your friendship, start working on those particular areas first. In other words, start *being* that friend. Then brick by brick, rebuild that friendship.

Take it from someone who's been there. You can build that friendship again, perhaps even stronger. Friendship doesn't happen by accident. You don't find yourself holding hands after twenty-five years with the one who you love by pure chance. Love is deliberate, it's intentional, it's purposeful, and in the end it's worth every minute that you give of yourself to another.

Marriage is a thousand little things. It's giving up your right to be *right* in the heat of an argument. It's forgiving another when he lets you down. It's loving someone enough to step down so he can shine. It's friendship. It's being a cheerleader and trusted confidante. It's a place of forgiveness that welcomes one home and arms he can run to in the midst of a storm. It's grace.

It's giving of yourself tirelessly down paths you never imagined you would travel. Through sickness and pain, poverty and loss, it's carrying the weight of another. It's being the smile he sees in the morning and the body he holds close at night. It's pure love. It's standing together in the face of adversity. It's riding alongside each other in a battle that threatens to tear down your marriage and seeks to grab hold of your faith. It's strength under pressure.

It's listening to the heart of another and understanding his pain. It's offering words of encouragement when he needs them most. It's walking hand in hand in the park and kissing gently in the pouring rain. It's laughing together.

A friend should be a place of safe retreat, where one can hide from the storm. But if you harbor resentment and anger, you can't possibly be the loyal friend that another will trust with his heart.

The embrace of a wife can be one of the most sacred

places on earth. It's a place of refuge where a husband can rest from the toil of everyday life. It's a place where he is welcome and wanted. He is strengthened by her gentle embrace and restored by her kindness. Her grace is the light that breaks through the darkness, streaming into his soul.

I want to be that woman. That friend. But I know that unless I'm willing to let go of anger, resentment, and hurt, I won't be that place of refuge. Even the slightest bit of resentment can seep into my thoughts and cause damage if I'm not walking in compassion and grace.

I'm reminded of the night that I noticed a little water on the kitchen floor by the sink, which is par for the course considering that most days Nathaniel spills far more than he drinks. I grabbed a tea towel and wiped up the spot. No problem. But when I went into the kitchen an hour later and noticed a bulging box of dishwasher detergent under the sink and another puddle of water beneath my feet, I knew we had a leak somewhere that had to be fixed. It wasn't too serious, but enough of a drip that I stood on towels to wash dishes and had to change my socks.

The sound of Michael tinkering in the kitchen after dinner was music to my ears. I wondered whether he might be too tired or too busy to get to it that evening, but since we both know that water can cause permanent damage if it's left to soak, he wanted to repair it right away.

See where I'm going with this? The Scriptures remind

us of yet another damaging drip—a contentious woman: "A continual dripping on a very rainy day / And a contentious woman are alike" (Prov. 27:15 NKJV). Contention appears in numerous ways, including opposing, nagging, arguing, challenging, belittling, and competing. And why do we do it? Because somehow we think that by nagging them we're encouraging our husbands to be better people. The truth is that many husbands—and many wives for that matter—have fragile egos that should be handled with care and respect.

In the same way that a leaky faucet can cause permanent damage, our words left unchecked can damage our relationships and cause resentment to grow. I can't imagine what the state of my kitchen would be if we let that faucet leak for ten years, but in some marriages that's what's happening. Sometimes the damage appears insurmountable. Giving up, the couple walk away. And we wonder why we're not friends anymore?

Friends encourage you. Friends cheer you on. Friends are there to support you. Friends listen to you. Friends have your back. Friends are truthful yet compassionate. Friends make you laugh. Proverbs said it this way: "A man that hath friends must shew himself friendly" (18:24).

"But," you might say, "I'm the only one who is putting any effort into this marriage. What about him?"

Certainly it takes the work of two people to form a strong marriage bond, but my advice to you is to concentrate on your share of the work and leave him to do his. And if you are praying for your marriage, you're definitely not the only one working on this. God is at work.

A best friend is a God thing, especially when that best friend is your husband. Isn't he worth the work?

THE CHALLENGE

Sit down and make a list of what you consider to be the characteristics of a good friend. Some of them will come from this chapter, and others might be drawn from past relationships. Once your list is complete, review it wisely. In what areas of your relationship is God calling you to grow? Talk it through with your husband. What are his thoughts? Bring it to prayer, asking God to guide your steps and strengthen your bond of friendship.

| THIRTEEN |

Be Content with the Life That You're Given

TWO SUMMERS AGO MY HUSBAND AND I took the kids on a road trip. It was the same trip that my parents took my sisters and me on when I was about eleven years old. We drove across Canada to Banff, Alberta, and I'd been itching to go back ever since. Banff was beautiful, but for me it was all about going back to Heritage Park in Calgary. While people dream about going to exotic places like Paris and Rome, I dream about the day when I can go back to Heritage Park. Call me a goof, but it's one of my favorite places on earth.

My guess is that it stems from my love of *Little House on the Prairie*. Growing up, I never missed an episode, and I still watch the reruns with my kids today. That Nellie Oleson and her wicked grin still get under my skin every time!

The first time we went to Heritage Park, the show was in its second season, and Walnut Grove was on everyone's lips. To visit a town that resembled it? That was a breathtaking experience.

The entire town is authentic. You can dine in the restaurant on the corner, visit the old schoolhouse, shop at the mercantile store, and hop a train from Heritage station. If I could live there I would—in a second. I'd grab a room above the mercantile where I could hammer away at an old typewriter while listening to the sound of horses clip-clopping outside my window. I think I'd be willing to give up the Internet for that, even if only a week. And I wouldn't mind wearing one of those apron dresses and bonnets either. If only they were back in style; today's fashion just doesn't compare, does it?

Michael, on the other hand, enjoyed Banff. He's the hiking/exploring type while I'm the shopping/spending type. So once we arrived in Banff, he took the boys exploring while Madison and I went shopping. I would go exploring with him, but I value my life too much. He likes to go off the beaten path and isn't afraid of what he might find. If you have to pack bear repellant, it's probably not the safest journey to take. That's my take on it.

We drove from Winnipeg, Manitoba, to Banff, Alberta, stopping in Regina and Calgary along the way. I offered to do some of the driving, but Michael insisted on staying behind the wheel while I caught up on my reading. It's amazing how fast you can go through a book when you're traveling, isn't it? I went through two.

Thankfully, before leaving home Michael picked up a GPS. It's a pretty cool little gadget to have, especially when you're traveling across country as we were.

Michael was enjoying his new toy, and after using it to navigate through the city of Calgary, we couldn't imagine traveling without it. The GPS was able to direct us from our driveway at home to the front door of our hotel without a hitch. It was awesome. That is, until we had a craving for Mexican food.

We live in a city with more than 700,000 people, but we're not well served when it comes to Mexican food. So whenever we visit a new city, we're always in search of good enchiladas. Usually, we can find a good Mexican restaurant without too much difficulty, but this night proved to be different. I don't know if Michael was tired that night or if Calgary was that confusing, but even *with* the GPS he managed to miss every turn.

Anytime you miss a turn, the voice on the GPS system says, "Recalculating," which is fine unless you're missing turns left, right, and center. Then it's more than annoying. The family was silent, Michael was tense, and the GPS was chanting, "Recalculating, recalculating, recalculating," until we finally arrived at the restaurant where we discovered a Closed sign. It was time to get back in the Jeep and recalculate things again.

A few weeks later, a friend pointed out to us how marriage is like a GPS system, and after that trip I could definitely relate. Most people go into marriage with an idea of what things should look like and how life will pan out. One of the most exciting things that you can do with your partner is to discuss your hopes and dreams for the future. We did it. Doesn't everybody?

When Michael and I were dating, we drew up plans for our dream home. We knew how many kids we wanted to have, where we wanted to live, and when we planned to retire. We even picked out a name for our dog, which we didn't have yet. We talked about the style of furniture we liked, the dishes we wanted, and the ways we'd celebrate holidays. Like other young couples, we programmed these things into our GPS system as we saved and planned for the future.

The problem—if you can even call it a problem—is that our lives are constantly recalculating the paths that we take. Since it's impossible to see past today, things rarely (if ever) turn out *exactly* the way that we planned. We didn't plan to have five miscarriages and then a sick baby, to endure sleepless nights, to deal with unemployment, or to buy a new company. All we are given is *this* moment; tomorrow belongs to the Lord. The question is, are we flexible enough to let Him lead the way? In other words, are we content when things don't go our way?

A contented woman brings glory to her husband while trusting God for her future. A discontented woman is the equivalent of a nagging GPS. Imagine for a moment that instead of happily recalculating the journey for you, a voice came over the system complaining, nagging, and reminding you that you missed every turn. How long do you think you'd listen to it before turning off the volume or tossing it out the window?

Recalculating is natural. It becomes a problem only when we stop trusting God with our futures. We have a choice: we can enjoy the twists and the turns in the road, or we can complain that life isn't all that we hoped it would be. The time comes when all of us have to choose.

One of my favorite examples of contentment is found in the story of Ruth. After the deaths of her husband and her two sons, Naomi decided to leave Moab and return to her homeland of Judah. But there was a special bond between Naomi and her daughter-in-law Ruth, a Moabite, who was determined to stay by her side.

Regardless of how difficult this transition could turn out to be for her, Ruth said, "Entreat me not to leave thee, or to return from following after thee: for whither thou goest, I will go; and where thou lodgest, I will lodge: thy people shall be my people, and thy God my God: where thou diest, will I die, and there will I be buried: the Lord do so to me, and more also, if ought but death part thee and me" (Ruth 1:16–17). Ruth didn't know what the future would hold, where she'd be sleeping, how they would support themselves, or whether she'd ever find another husband. There was a strong possibility that the people would not accept her; the Moabites had a long history of conflict with the Israelites. But Ruth was willing to trust God with her future. None of us can tell what the future holds, which is why it's so important to possess that same faithful attitude when planning and dreaming ahead.

Ask yourself, *Will I be content if God changes my plans?* And challenge yourself to be so when things don't go your way.

Here's a quotation from a familiar voice that echoes my thoughts: "'This earthly life is a battle,' said Ma. 'If it isn't one thing to contend with, it's another. It always has been so, and it always will be. The sooner you make up your mind to that, the better off you are, and more thankful for your pleasures.'"[1]

I think a big part of the reason that so many people like me have fallen in love with the Little House stories and in particular the character of Caroline Ingalls is her gentleness and contentment. She's an example to many. As a pioneer woman in the 1800s, she struggled alongside her husband to make ends meet and raise their five children. Not only did this woman make do with the little they had; she did it gracefully. Time and again they battled against the elements of nature, never knowing how their next crop would turn out, and when they did face trouble, she looked past it to thank God for their blessings.

Contentment requires us to trade personal and immediate gratification for a heightened sense of appreciation. That kind of faith can be difficult, but those who choose to "let go and let God" possess a gem of great worth.

We're not used to seeing that in this world. The media conditions us to want more, expect more, and anticipate more. When circumstances don't reward us the way we hoped that they would, we patiently wait, dream, and imagine what life will be like when we finally reach the island of "more." What we should be doing is stopping to thank God for *this* moment before moving on to the next: "In everything give thanks: for this is the will of God in Christ Jesus concerning you" (1 Thess. 5:18).

Patience is good, but contentment calls us to take a step further in faith, which is why the two should be working together. Contentment doesn't wish that today was tomorrow. Contentment lives in each present moment with an attitude of gratitude. The reward is at hand. It isn't an easy choice, but the best things in life never are.

I knew of one husband who wanted to be a carpenter early on in his marriage. Not having a garage, he set up a table saw in the bedroom of their little apartment and built cabinets there. No, he didn't clean up after himself. His wife vacuumed the sawdust and moved his tools off the bed at night.

I don't know how many women would handle that as patiently as she did. Her kind and gentle spirit draws him close to her side, and after thirty years they are still happily married. He now has a big garage for his tools and has since built her a beautiful kitchen. By looking past his faults, she is able to see a kind, generous man and amazing father with a heart that's bigger than his garage ever could be.

But if he wasn't that man? If he wasn't so kind and generous, what then? By drawing him close and captivating his heart, his wife has the power to influence him. It's an influence that would otherwise be lost if she pushed him away. Peter urged, "Ye wives, be in subjection to your own husbands; that, if any obey not the word, they also may without the word be won by the conversation of the wives" (1 Peter 3:1).

Be thankful for where you are in your marriage *today*. Finances might be tight, his habits might grate on your nerves, or you might sense that the romance is gone. All that could very well be true, but there's a fine gem waiting to be held in the palm of your hand. Hold on to contentment; the reward is at hand. "Rejoice evermore. Pray without ceasing. In every thing give thanks: for this is the will of God in Christ Jesus concerning you" (1 Thess. 5:16–18).

Here's a letter that I received from a widow who was urging us to appreciate our husbands while we still have them.

Dear Darlene,

I went into marriage with the storybook idea of living happily ever after. When my "knight in shining armor" turned out to be just a local peasant, I turned bitter. I was constantly on his case trying to change him into the person I wanted him to be. Every little thing he did that displeased me became blown out of proportion, and I made sure to point his faults out constantly.

I went through years of hell wishing I had never married him and wishing he were someone else. I never really took a good long look at myself or saw what a nag I had become. I got angry when others would say how "hen pecked" my husband had become, and I would think that they didn't really know this man like I did.

When Jesus came into my life, I began to see my faults and to change a lot of my actions. I finally learned to live in contentment and be thankful for the great man I had. I couldn't believe how my husband stood by me all of those years.

Suddenly my husband passed away after 35 years of marriage, and now I am alone.

I am writing this in the hopes that some of the younger women will change their minds and attitudes before it's too late. For every fault you see in your husband, you will find as many, or more, in yourself. Learn to be content with what you have and build on that foundation.

The funny thing is that those little things he used to do—the things that would annoy me so much—are the things that I miss the most now. I miss him leaving his clothes lying around. I miss him taking so much time in the bathroom. I miss having to clean up after him. But most of all—I miss him.

I wish I could have started out my marriage with God in control, because I wouldn't have so many regrets today.

We don't realize what we have till it is taken from us.

Sincerely,

The Aged

Are you a Caroline Ingalls, or do you tend to have more days when things get under your skin and you find yourself saying, "Why me?" We all know how it is; it seems that the minute everything is going along great, it starts falling apart. And then there are other times when, like Job, you seem to have one trouble after another and start to wonder if things will ever let up.

Living in Canada, I can't help being reminded of our bitter-cold winters. They are long and harsh. Just running to the store to pick up a jug of milk is a huge undertaking. We have to let the car warm up for a while, scrape the car windows, bundle up for the ride, and depending on the recent snowfall, we might have to shovel the vehicle out of the driveway. During those months I wonder if we'll ever enjoy another hot summer day.

It's really hard to imagine, but sure enough the snow eventually melts, and the flowers bloom again.

It's hard to look past the moment. Irritations, whether big or small, have a way of spoiling an otherwise beautiful day, don't they? Even when you believe that things are bound to turn around, it's difficult to look up.

So how do we fix it? How can we make our world a better place so that we'll be happy within it? The answer is that we can't and we shouldn't expect to.

There will be days when you wake up on the wrong side of the bed and wish you could crawl back in. There will be people who disappoint you so badly that all you're left with are the shattered pieces of your heart. There will be pain, there will be loss, and there will be tears. But God in His wisdom is good. Joy comes from within, not without.

Have you ever wondered why God cursed Adam and Eve? Here are His words:

Unto the woman he said, I will greatly multiply thy sorrow and thy conception; in sorrow thou shalt bring forth children; and thy desire shall be to thy husband, and he shall rule over thee. And unto Adam he said, Because thou hast hearkened unto the voice of thy wife, and hast eaten of the tree, of which I commanded thee, saying, Thou shalt not eat of it: cursed is the ground for thy sake; in sorrow shalt thou eat of it all the days of thy life; thorns also and

179

thistles shall it bring forth to thee; and thou shalt eat the herb of the field; In the sweat of thy face shalt thou eat bread, till thou return unto the ground; for out of it wast thou taken: for dust thou art, and unto dust shalt thou return. (Gen. 3:16–19)

We know that the Curse is the result of man's sin. Why then are we, who are forgiven of sin, still living under the Curse? Because the Curse is a constant reminder that we are in desperate need of salvation. It was designed with a purpose—put there for our good—so that we might understand our need for a Savior.

God is treating us as dear children, and like a true Father, He disciplines us for our good. It's never pleasant at the time, but with each trial we grow more disciplined, and we learn. The more that we take our focus off the things of this world, we turn our hearts and our minds toward God.

My problem was that every time I faced disappointment, I focused on the world, assuming that the grass was greener beyond my fence. I was looking outward for a solution when the real issue was that I needed to grow in contentment, forgiveness, understanding, and love. When we run from our problems, we don't learn to solve them. But when we patiently trust God with our hearts, He leads us safely through to the other side. Not necessarily *comfortably*, but safely nonetheless.

I haven't arrived yet. But then again no one has. Marriage

is a lifelong journey that leads us to grow every step of the way. I'm still walking in faith, but my focus is on the Lord.

We can't change the world around us completely, but we can change the way we relate to it so that while we're riding the waves, we keep an even keel. All too often we have that reversed. We spend all our energy focused on changing our surroundings so that we'll feel better, happier, contented, and relaxed—when the reality is that this peace comes from within.

The sooner we learn to let go and let God take the wheel, the sooner we start enjoying the ride.

THE CHALLENGE

The next time things don't go as planned, choose joy. Your initial reaction might be one of disappointment, but you have the ability to turn that around and thank God in the moment. If your husband is doing things his way? If he's not living according to plan? Handle things wisely, communicate your desire in love, and avoid any temptation to nag.

FOURTEEN

Walk in Virtue According to Wisdom

MICHAEL HAS THE PATIENCE OF JOB. SOME days I wish that I had even a fraction of his patience. And the temperance. And the kindness. And the humility. The man's not perfect—don't get me wrong—but he often reminds me that virtue is a beautiful thing.

It was Mother's Day. The sun was shining, the smell of spring was in the air, and according to Michael I had some shopping to do. Not only did I need to pick up a little something for my mother (yeah, I tend to procrastinate), he also wanted me to pick up a few clothes for myself.

Shortly after lunch we hopped into the Jeep and went for a drive. Since his back wasn't feeling so great, Michael wanted to stay in the car while my daughter and I ran into the store. He didn't mind if we took awhile as long as I found something I liked.

Unfortunately, it wasn't as easy as all that. After trying on shirt after shirt, I decided that nothing I liked was worth buying. A few things fit, but I wasn't about to walk around town looking like Midlife Crisis Barbie. I needed something modest and comfortable. It was difficult being so picky when I knew that my husband was waiting patiently outside in the Jeep.

Finally I got back to the vehicle, hopped in my seat with a smile on my face, and said, "Thanks for waiting. That was a lot of fun!" Truth be told, it wasn't a *lot* of fun. It started out that way but became a frustrating experience. I was trying to muster up the best attitude I could. After all, he had been waiting about forty-five minutes.

Taking one look at me, Michael said, "You didn't pick up anything for yourself, did you?"

"Um, no," I answered, "but that's totally fine. I get things all the time!"

Insisting that I find something nice, he drove across town and parked in the box-store parking lot. In our city, this is considered the cream of the crop for clothes shopping. Surrounded by clothing stores, anyone and everyone will likely find *something* to wear. I guess I'm not anyone or everyone because after about another hour and a half, I was still empty-handed. Madison was making out just fine. She found too many outfits.

Again I went back to the hot car without a purchase. Michael gave me *the look*. "Still nothing?"

I was worn out, and I told him so. I didn't want to struggle with yet another top that I couldn't pull over my head or a pair of pants that I couldn't zip up. I really wanted to give up. After all, he had been sitting in the car all afternoon. This was getting ridiculous on my part. Surely he wanted to leave.

Driving out of the lot, he spotted a shop that neither of us had ever stepped foot in. As far as I knew, it was an old-lady store. I might be struggling with my weight, and I am getting close to fifty, but I'm not ready for elastic-waist pants that pull up to my chest.

"Humor me," he said. "Please, just one more?"

I don't know anyone who would be willing to sit in the hot sun doing absolutely nothing for several hours while his wife goes inside shopping for clothes. Seriously? How could I even think of torturing this man for another minute?

"Please," he insisted. And he pulled into the lot where he parked in front of the store. "One more try."

I not only found a store that was well stocked in my size; I discovered that it had some pretty cute clothes. I picked up two skirts, a couple of T-shirts, and a lightweight denim jacket. I walked out of that store with a smile on my face and two shopping bags in hand. Michael's patience paid off.

Patience is a virtue that's not easy to come by, at least not for me. But then again good things rarely come easily, do they?

Walking in virtue is a struggle that we face every day. Whether we're talking about patience, kindness, forgiveness, or humility, we're called to lay down our desires for the good of another: "As God's chosen people, holy and dearly loved, clothe yourselves with compassion, kindness, humility, gentleness and patience. Bear with each other and forgive one another if any of you has a grievance against someone. Forgive as the Lord forgave you. And over all these virtues put on love, which binds them all together in perfect unity" (Col. 3:12–14 NIV).

We've all heard of the virtuous woman described in Proverbs 31, and we all know that patience is a virtue, but what does the word really mean? Another question might be: what is the difference between good *values* and *virtues*? Seeing the difference between the two and the importance of virtue helps me not only to understand Scripture but also to take the necessary steps to apply it to my life.

Values vary from person to person according to his or her cultural upbringing, social standing, and adherence to faith. They are the things that we deem important, such as valuing friendships and honesty.

Virtues refer to "conformity to a standard of right: morality."[1] The key word is *conformity*. Christian virtues are evident in our living by the wisdom of God. Not perfectly as we're all growing in grace, but we should be building our faith upon them daily. The most common Christian virtues are purity, benevolence (desire toward goodwill), diligence, patience, kindness, and humility, and there are many others.

Before we talk more about virtue, we should also talk about knowledge because it's so important that the two of them go hand in hand: "Beside this, giving all diligence, add to your faith virtue; and to virtue knowledge" (2 Peter 1:5). When we walk in virtue, we declare God's glory to the world. We become beacons of light in the darkness. But in order to do that we must start with seeking the will of God through prayer and searching the Scriptures. That's where we find direction. As the psalmist wrote, "Thy word is a lamp unto my feet, and a light unto my path" (Ps. 119:105).

If we watch talk shows hoping to gain marital advice or search the Internet seeking answers, we're being spoon-fed by society. We may find something of use, yes, but unless we're able to compare it to the truth found in Scripture, we can easily be led astray. In fact this often happens.

Even more damaging are the seemingly intelligent people who offer advice to Christians based on a secular view rather than biblical principles. It's more damaging because we are trusting, and those who are weak in the faith can be easily swayed.

"You deserve to be happy!" That sounds pretty good

coming from a woman with a PhD, stylishly coifed hair, and well-manicured nails, never mind the fact that her life isn't anywhere close to being in line with God's Word. She might have some values, but let's not confuse values with Christian virtue. Go to the Scriptures for guidance, and if you still need direction, speak to someone you know who is walking in virtue and truth.

God seeks an *eternal* plan for your life and understands the blessings that come with self-sacrifice. Living in glory and virtue says that our lives, our choices, and our conduct will be lined up with the principles laid out in the Bible, not the messages that society is tossing our way.

It's so easy to get caught up in the mind-set of pop culture. I know that I did for a time. We tell ourselves that God wants us to be happy, and so we make decisions based on a temporal high and ignore God's bigger plan for our souls. That way of thinking led me into a place of darkness and despair that I pray you never find. God offers joy and peace to those who are exercised by obedience. That's much different from seeking happiness regardless of the cost. Faith says that I'm going to put my trust in Him whether it feels like I'm walking on glass or soaking my feet at the spa. That's what determines virtue.

There's a lot of talk in our society about trophy wives. *Groan.* Some men pursue young, attractive women as status symbols. But holy men of God know that there is much more to a woman than her outer appearance. Proverbs 12:4 tells us that "a virtuous woman is a crown to her husband." In other words, she is a treasure.

After Michael waited for me all afternoon while I shopped, I realized that his patience and kindness were the real gift—not the clothing. The shopping was an extension of his love for me, but he displayed the root of his love through his virtue. A gift like that can't be bought in a box store. That's what makes it so precious.

Let's explore the example of this virtuous woman in Proverbs 31 to see what she brought to her marriage and how we can apply those elements to our lives:

1. She was trustworthy.

"The heart of her husband doth safely trust in her, so that he shall have no need of spoil" (v. 11). I've always loved this verse, but even more so when I recently considered the meaning behind it. "Have no need of spoil." What does that mean? *Spoil* is a word often found in the Old Testament to describe the loot that armies divided among themselves after they won a battle. It was a reward that each soldier could take home to his wife.

Such times are good. We like a little bonus check, don't we? Financial concerns, however, are common issues of contention in marriage. It's a major cause of worry, stress, discontentment, and divorce.

A husband who trusts his wife knows that she won't walk

away from the marriage when times are tough. He knows that she values the commitment she made and will be there through good times and bad.

2. She was kind and considerate.

"She will do him good and not evil all the days of her life" (v. 12). It should go without saying that two people in love will treat each other with kindness and consideration. But in many marriages that's not the case because people would rather hang on to their anger and hurt than walk in humility.

Our husbands will let us down, and there will be days when they get under our skin, but the way that we choose to relate to them in times of stress will speak volumes about our character.

3. She worked willingly.

"She seeketh wool, and flax, and worketh willingly with her hands" (v. 13). This woman wasn't only working with her hands; she was *willingly* working. How many of us can say that about the laundry we do? Are we doing it just because it *has* to be done, or can we find joy in doing it because we are bringing a gift to the family?

We read in verse 16 that she bought a field and planted a vineyard. She also worked *hard*.

4. She was diligent.

"She is like the merchants' ships; she bringeth her food from afar" (v. 14). I chose the word *diligent* because I see someone who makes a conscious effort to feed her family. Are we willing to go the extra mile to make sure that the family eats well? Or will we be tempted to take the fast-food approach? Of course, this is only one example of diligence, but it shows the importance of effort.

If you've gotten this far in the chapter, you might be thinking, *Slow the roll! How can I possibly keep up with the perfection of the Proverbs 31 woman?* Now, before you become discouraged, start hating her, and close the book, let me assure you that *none* of us can. She is a standard of perfection and excellence.

We must strive to be diligent, yes, and it's important that we're trustworthy and kind, but in the midst of all our failures and imperfections, we are made perfect through nothing but faith in Jesus Christ. It's for this reason that Jesus said, "My yoke is easy, and my burden is light" (Matt. 11:30). He is the One who carried the burden of your imperfection. It was nailed to the cross along with Him.

God doesn't expect us to be perfect; He just wants to see us growing in grace. Growing means that we'll be in pursuit of perfect virtue, not necessarily in *possession* of it. While you are growing in grace, remember that He loved you long before you loved Him.

5. She was self-controlled.

"She riseth also while it is yet night, and giveth meat to her household, and a portion to her maidens" (v. 15). When we think of virtuous women, we often picture them as being loving, generous, and kind; they reach their hands out to the poor, lead their children in faith, and provide food for their families. I tend to overlook that virtuous women also exhibit a high level of self-control.

I'm not a morning person, so I can't begin to tell you just how impressed I am with this. I'm sure if I was sitting down to have tea with her, I'd ask, "What? You get up at what time?"

I practically said that exact thing today when I was chatting with one of my neighbors. She has the most obedient, fun-loving dog I've ever seen. He's a big teddy bear. The minute he sees you, Willis will flip over on his back and wait for a belly scratch. I love that guy!

Today I noticed that he doesn't as much as flinch when another dog walks by. He's always outside without a leash and never leaves her side unless it's for a belly rub.

"How did you get so lucky?" I asked as I bent down to scratch his tummy.

"Oh, it wasn't luck," she said. "We got him at six weeks old, and for the first month I got up every morning an hour earlier than the kids to train him. I'd take him outside and show him where his boundaries were and what we expected of him. I had to be on him 24/7."

I had already thought this woman was pretty much perfect in every way, but this one cinched it. She cooks like Rachael Ray, decorates like Martha Stewart, and works out like Jillian Michaels. Now she's got a dog that puts Lassie to shame. It's no wonder her husband is always smiling. She has three kids and looks like a teenager, but I still love her.

Getting up is one thing, but we're really talking about the virtue of self-control. We're all a work in progress as we strive to put *will* over *want*. Whether we're talking about satisfying our appetites, overspending, being lazy, or losing our tempers, we all benefit from exercising the virtue of self-control.

If you value a clean home, do the grunt work it takes to get there. If you value your faith, nurture it by opening your Bible more often and taking time out to pray. If you value your marriage, actively work on your relationship.

Whatever you're struggling with, make every effort to be self-controlled. That's when you'll notice results!

6. She was compassionate.

"She stretcheth out her hand to the poor; yea, she reacheth forth her hands to the needy" (v. 20). It's easy enough to write a check and throw 10 percent in the offering basket at church every week; what isn't so easy is reaching our hands out to the people around us.

Here is an example of compassion. She made an effort to reach out to people, not just put something in their pocketbooks. My guess is that she got to know people in need and lent a hand when she could.

Compassion is one of the most beautiful virtues that a woman can possess in that she reflects God's love to the world.

7. She was well kempt.

"She maketh herself coverings of tapestry; her clothing is silk and purple" (v. 22).

I've come to learn that faith and family are the two most important things to Michael, and I also know that he loves me whether I'm dressed to the nines or I'm walking around the house with a chip clip in my hair and two socks that don't match. He's faithful that way.

But here's the problem: that knowledge and the level of comfort in our relationship offer me the opportunity to be lazier than I should be. In other words there's a temptation to take his love for granted.

Some days this translates into me walking around like a slob, whereas the flip side of that is when I put in the extra effort to treasure the person he is.

I'm not saying that wives should walk around the house

like pageant queens with big hair and high heels complementing their stunning dresses. By all means, be true to yourself and the woman you are in Christ. I'm merely saying that we should offer our husbands respect in the way that we act and the way that we dress, exerting the effort when and where we can.

Is it self-seeking to want a loving and devoted husband who is proud to call you his wife? Definitely not. While other men may complain about their wives, a man has a sense of pride to know his wife is different. She's unique; she understands him when no one else does; she looks up to him as her protector and the one who provides; she has admirable character that he can trust.

When you're a radiant bride that your husband is proud to call his, you are worth far more than rubies; you are his crown.

THE CHALLENGE

If you aren't doing so already, start reading the Bible daily. Even if it's just a chapter each day, you need to be in the Word in order to discover God's will for your life. If you are looking for short Bible studies that might help you along, I offer free ones through my website at www .darleneschacht.net.

| FIFTEEN |

Pray for Your Marriage

I WANDERED THROUGH THE AIRPORT FOL-
lowing sign after sign until I finally arrived at the baggage
carousel. It had been four nights and five days. I was ready
for home.

Examining each black suitcase that passed my way, I
asked myself, *Darlene, why haven't you tied a pink scarf to the
handle?* Every time we travel, I ask myself that question, and
every time I get home, I forget about the pink scarf that hangs
in the closet. It's adorable by the way.

Finally hoisting my bag over the edge, I was ready to
go. Within the hour I'd embrace four inquisitive children I

197

missed dearly, two pugs that would surely lick my face, and a husband who can best be described as home to my heart.

I walked through the doors of the airport where center stage was the orange Jeep with its engine running as if it were waiting for mama to come home. Standing beside the Jeep was a servant's heart, clothed in blue jeans with arms outstretched. And beneath that cold October sky I embraced the warm feeling of home.

Stepping into my house, I discovered that the past four days had rested in the hands of a capable husband and father. I was warmly reminded of how my Savior once rose from the table to wash twenty-four feet.

The smell of bleach and the sight of warm smiles from kids with clean faces told me that they had been tenderly cared for. What I found also told me that Michael was loving his wife as Christ loved the church and gave Himself for it. What more could I ask for? What more could I possibly want?

When I get to thinking that way another question arises, *What can I give in return?* I can clean up the house today and toss a few loads of laundry in before he gets home. I might even cook his favorite dinner, but a long-lasting gift—and one that should never be taken lightly—is the gift of prayer.

I know that some of you really have it together when it comes to prayer. You can pray over a Big Mac as eloquently as one would thank God for filet mignon. I'm not that way. In fact I'm one fry short of a Happy Meal when it comes to saying the right thing.

I've knelt through prayer meetings thinking about everything *but* prayer, and then I remind myself that I'm supposed to be concentrating on the Lord. I shuffle my position and get official until my thoughts drift off once again. Praise God for His unfailing grace on this cracked vessel. How great is His patience with me!

I see a different picture of prayer when I visualize King David—one that's far less about self and far more about God: "Seven times a day do I praise thee because of thy righteous judgments. Great peace have they which love thy law: and nothing shall offend them" (Ps. 119:164–65). Those words move me to say, "More of You, Lord, less of me."

What might that look like in a wife who desires to bring life to her marriage?

Could this be a picture of me praying by the kitchen sink while I'm washing my dishes? It could be. And, yes, the Lord assures me that my eyes might be open as I take in the view from the backyard. I see the trees that my husband and I planted together, and I praise God for His gift of a husband.

Could this be a picture of me praising the Lord as I snuggle in close to my husband at night? What about that quiet moment in the afternoon when I'm folding his laundry?

Home is the tapestry I weave day in and day out, and prayer is the loom upon which I place my thread. Every prayer is a gift of love I stitch into the lives of my husband and children. Paul encouraged us to pray, saying, "Be careful for nothing; but in every thing by prayer and supplication with thanksgiving let your requests be made known unto God" (Phil. 4:6). I'm forever learning that prayer has everything to do with the Lord and nothing to do with my righteousness. Righteousness is imputed to us by faith. We merely need to seek Him with a pure heart.

This book started with prayer, and I can't think of a better way to close it than by continuing that journey long after you turn the last page. I pray that together we'll continue to seek Him in all that we do with a desire to strengthen our marriages and build them upon a strong foundation of faith.

It's by grace that I wrote this book, and through His grace I share my testimony with you so that you may see how one cracked vessel was lifted from a pit of sin and shame by the hand of an almighty God who offers hope for tomorrow.

Patience and self-sacrifice are grievous for a time, but they bring peace to those who are exercised by them. And so we must continue steadfast in the Lord, trusting Him every step of the way.

I challenge you as I challenge myself to draw closer to Him by equipping ourselves with the gospel, taking time out for prayer, and walking according to His will, not ours. I pray that we will hunger for more than lukewarm marriages and halfhearted faith by pursuing God with all our hearts.

That's how we equip ourselves for the ministry of leading our children and supporting our husbands. Amen?

And so I'd like to offer you thirty-one prayers for your marriage. That's one for every day of the month. If you'd like a free printable, I have created small prayer cards that you can hang on a ring and keep in your purse or on your nightstand. You can find them at www.darleneschacht.net.

31 Prayers for My Marriage

1. That we will draw closer to God.

    "Draw nigh to God, and he will draw nigh to you. Cleanse your hands, ye sinners; and purify your hearts, ye double minded" (James 4:8).

2. That we will grow in wisdom.

    "Wisdom is the principal thing; therefore get wisdom: and with all thy getting get understanding" (Prov. 4:7).

3. That we will stand strong against everything that threatens to tear our marriage apart or pull us away from the Lord.

    "My brethren, be strong in the Lord, and in the power of his might. Put on the whole armour of God, that ye may be able to stand against the wiles of the devil. For we wrestle not against flesh and blood, but against principalities, against powers, against the rulers of the darkness of this world, against spiritual wickedness in high places" (Eph. 6:10–12).

4. That we will be wise parents.

"Ye fathers, provoke not your children to wrath: but bring them up in the nurture and admonition of the Lord" (Eph. 6:4).

5. That our faith will increase.

"The Lord said, If ye had faith as a grain of mustard seed, ye might say unto this sycamine tree, Be thou plucked up by the root, and be thou planted in the sea; and it should obey you" (Luke 17:6).

6. That we will trust God through every trial.

"Trust in the LORD with all thine heart; and lean not unto thine own understanding. In all thy ways acknowledge him, and he shall direct thy paths" (Prov. 3:5–6).

7. That we will keep our eyes on the Lord.

"The peace of God, which passeth all understanding, shall keep your hearts and minds through Christ Jesus" (Phil. 4:7).

8. That we will maintain good health.

"Pleasant words are as an honeycomb, sweet to the soul, and health to the bones" (Prov. 16:24).

9. That our marriage will be a godly example to others.

"Let no man despise thy youth; but be thou an example of the believers, in word, in conversation, in charity, in spirit, in faith, in purity" (1 Tim. 4:12).

10. That we will seek God with pure and humble hearts.

"If from thence thou shalt seek the LORD thy God, thou shalt find him, if thou seek him with all thy heart and with all thy soul" (Deut. 4:29).

11. That we will have compassion for the world around us.

"Put on therefore, as the elect of God, holy and beloved, bowels of mercies, kindness, humbleness of mind, meekness, longsuffering; forbearing one another, and forgiving one another, if any man have a quarrel against any: even as Christ forgave you, so also do ye. And above all these things put on charity, which is the bond of perfectness" (Col. 3:12–14).

12. That we will walk faithfully, redeeming the time.

"Unto whomsoever much is given, of him shall be much required: and to whom men have committed much, of him they will ask the more" (Luke 12:48).

13. That we will be content with little or with much.

"We brought nothing into this world, and it is certain we can carry nothing out. And having food and raiment let us be therewith content" (1 Tim. 6:7–8).

14. That we will run to God in times of trouble.

"He that dwelleth in the secret place of the most High shall abide under the shadow of the Almighty. I will say of the LORD, He is my refuge and my fortress: my God; in him will I trust" (Ps. 91:1–2).

15. That our prayer life will be strengthened.

     "In every thing give thanks: for this is the will of God in Christ Jesus concerning you" (1 Thess. 5:18).

16. That we will live according to God's plan for our marriage.

     "As the church is subject unto Christ, so let the wives be to their own husbands in every thing. Husbands, love your wives, even as Christ also loved the church, and gave himself for it" (Eph. 5:24–25).

17. That we will be obedient to the will of God.

     "Be ye doers of the word, and not hearers only, deceiving your own selves. For if any be a hearer of the word, and not a doer, he is like unto a man beholding his natural face in a glass: For he beholdeth himself, and goeth his way, and straightway forgetteth what manner of man he was" (James 1:22–24).

18. That we will walk in humility.

     "He riseth from supper, and laid aside his garments; and took a towel, and girded himself. After that he poureth water into a bason, and began to wash the disciples' feet, and to wipe them with the towel wherewith he was girded" (John 13:4–5).

19. That we will be united.

     "I therefore, the prisoner of the Lord, beseech you that ye walk worthy of the vocation wherewith ye are called, with all lowliness and meekness, with longsuffering, forbearing one another in love; endeavouring to keep the unity of the Spirit in the bond of peace" (Eph. 4:1–3).

20. That we will communicate wisely.

"Let no corrupt communication proceed out of your mouth, but that which is good to the use of edifying, that it may minister grace unto the hearers" (Eph. 4:29).

21. That serving God will be our first priority.

"If ye then be risen with Christ, seek those things which are above, where Christ sitteth on the right hand of God" (Col. 3:1).

22. That God will shape my role as a wife.

"That they may teach the young women to be sober, to love their husbands, to love their children, to be discreet, chaste, keepers at home, good, obedient to their own husbands, that the word of God be not blasphemed" (Titus 2:4–5).

23. That we will have hearts of gratitude.

"I will bless the LORD at all times: his praise shall continually be in my mouth" (Ps. 34:1).

24. That we will walk in virtue.

"Beside this, giving all diligence, add to your faith virtue; and to virtue knowledge; and to knowledge temperance; and to temperance patience; and to patience godliness; and to godliness brotherly kindness; and to brotherly kindness charity. For if these things be in you, and abound, they make you that ye shall neither be barren nor unfruitful in the knowledge of our Lord Jesus Christ" (2 Peter 1:5–8).

25. That our characters will reflect our faith.

"The fruit of the Spirit is love, joy, peace, longsuffering, gentleness, goodness, faith" (Gal. 5:22).

26. That we will hunger and thirst for the Word of God.

"As the hart panteth after the water brooks, so panteth my soul after thee, O God. My soul thirsteth for God, for the living God: when shall I come and appear before God?" (Ps. 42:1–2).

27. That our faith will be sincere and genuine.

"The end of the commandment is charity out of a pure heart, and of a good conscience, and of faith unfeigned" (1 Tim. 1:5).

28. That God will put a hedge of protection around our marriage.

"He that dwelleth in the secret place of the most High shall abide under the shadow of the Almighty. I will say of the LORD, He is my refuge and my fortress: my God; in him will I trust" (Ps. 91:1–2).

29. That we will fellowship with other believers and meet like-minded Christian couples.

"Let us consider one another to provoke unto love and to good works: not forsaking the assembling of

ourselves together, as the manner of some is; but exhort-
ing one another: and so much the more, as ye see the day
approaching" (Heb. 10:24–25).

30. That we will guide and nurture the growth of our children.

"Train up a child in the way he should go: and when
he is old, he will not depart from it" (Prov. 22:6).

31. That our lives and our words will be a testimony of our
faith.

"He said unto them, Go ye into all the world, and
preach the gospel to every creature" (Mark 16:15).

THE CHALLENGE

*Will you remember to pray for your marriage, or will you
forget after closing this book? I challenge you to tie a pink
scarf (or whatever color you have) to the oven door as a
constant reminder to whisper a prayer here and there.
When he asks you what that's all about, you can say,
"This one's for you, honey!"*

Acknowledgments

LORD JESUS, MY SAVIOR AND FRIEND, ONE day I'm failing grade-twelve English, and the next thing you know, I'm writing a book. If I've come to learn anything in my life, it's that all things are possible when they're placed in Your almighty hands. I have this Friend who's not only the God who rules over this entire universe and beyond but also is compassionate enough to walk by my side, offering grace each step of the way. Thank You from the bottom of my heart for Your unfailing grace.

Michael, my best friend this side of heaven, thank you for catching me when I fell. Your strength and grace are gifts that

209

rescued me from a pit of desperation and sin. Bold is the man who lets his wife write a book about the most intimate details of their lives and encourages her through the process. Thank you for being the lover and friend that you are.

Brendan, Madison, Graham, and Nathaniel, thank you for your prayers and your patience. We're told in Scripture that a wife of noble character is crown to her husband, and there is no doubt in my heart that you are the gems in this crown. Some of the greatest moments of my life have been spent behind the wheel of our car listening to the four of you laugh. You make this momma's heart sing. Thank you.

Matt, you are the dot to my *i*, the cross to my *t*. Thank you for believing in me. Thank you for walking me through this process. And thank you for your wisdom, without which I'd be lost. You are the backbone to this journey. The count-less hours that you have spent on this project have not gone unnoticed. You're an incredible agent and a man of strong faith and integrity, which are vital to me as a fellow believer. This publishing world is far more than just shuffling papers and reading the fine print. To me it's about being a vessel of faith that God can use for His glory. Thank you for being that man. Thank you for being my friend.

Lisa, no one has encouraged me through this process quite as much as you have. What is the count now, three thousand e-mails between us? There's rarely a day, if any at all, that I don't find a note of encouragement in my inbox.

You are a noble woman of character and a very dear friend. Thank you.

Soul sisters, Courtney, Angela, Ruth, Janelle, Clare, and Joy, one of the greatest blessings of this writing journey has been the opportunity of making some incredible friends. I love how God has brought us together and how He keeps bringing us back together time and again. That's pretty cool. Thank you all for your encouragement and for welcoming this old lady into your fold.

Thomas Nelson, what can I say but "wow"? Thank you from the bottom of my heart for believing in this book and standing behind it the way that you have. I count it among my greatest blessings to be a part of your family.

Notes

Chapter Three: Be Patient and Kind When the Going Gets Tough

1. Quoted in Malcolm Muggeridge, *Something Beautiful for God* (New York: HarperCollins, 1986), 113–14.

Chapter Eight: Communicate with Loving Respect

1. Anna Esposito, ed., *Fundamentals of Verbal and Nonverbal Communication and the Biometric Issue* (Amsterdam: IOS Press, 2007), 85.

Chapter Nine: Be the Woman Your Husband Needs You to Be

1. John Eldredge, *Captivating Heart to Heart Participant's Guide* (Nashville: Thomas Nelson, 2007), 54.
2. Ibid.

3. Louann Brizendine, *The Female Brain* (New York: Random House, 2007), 160.

Chapter Ten: Be Affectionate in Ways That Are Pleasing to God
1. Benedict Carey, "Evidence That Little Touches Do Mean So Much," *New York Times*, February 22, 2010.
2. Ibid.

Chapter Eleven: Seize the Day and Capture the Joy
1. Nicole, "What if You Didn't Have 'One More Time'?" September 9, 2012, http://indulgentaromas.blogspot.com/.
2. "Mother Teresa of Calcutta," biographical sketch, http://www.vatican.va/news_services/liturgy/saints/ ns_lit_doc_20031019_madre-teresa_en.html.
3. Cited in Bob Kelly, *Worth Repeating* (Grand Rapids: Kregel, 2003), 26.

Chapter Thirteen: Be Content with the Life That You're Given
1. Laura Ingalls Wilder, *Little Town on the Prairie* (New York: HarperCollins, 1971), 107–8.

Chapter Fourteen: Walk in Virtue According to Wisdom
1. *Merriam-Webster's Collegiate Dictionary*, 11th ed., s.v. "virtue."

About the Author

DARLENE SCHACHT'S WRITING TALENT, laced with design skill and determination, has placed her at the hub of online ministry where she has the ability to reach out to women in order to share faith and to minister to them. As the original founder of *Christian Women Online* magazine and the Internet Café Devotions, she is considered a pioneer among many of her peers. She has a strong online presence and the demonstrated ability to motivate women. Her popular blog, *Time-Warp Wife*, audience continues to show rapid growth.

She is the coauthor of Candace Cameron Bure's *New York Times* best-selling book, *Reshaping It All: Motivation for Physical and Spiritual Fitness.* Awards for *Reshaping It All* include 2011 USA Best Book Award and Christian Retailing 2012 Retailers Choice Award.

Darlene has been married to Michael Schacht for more than twenty-five years, and together they have four children. They are part of the faith community in Winnipeg, Manitoba.